# A Retrospective Look:
# The Artwork of R. L. Oliver

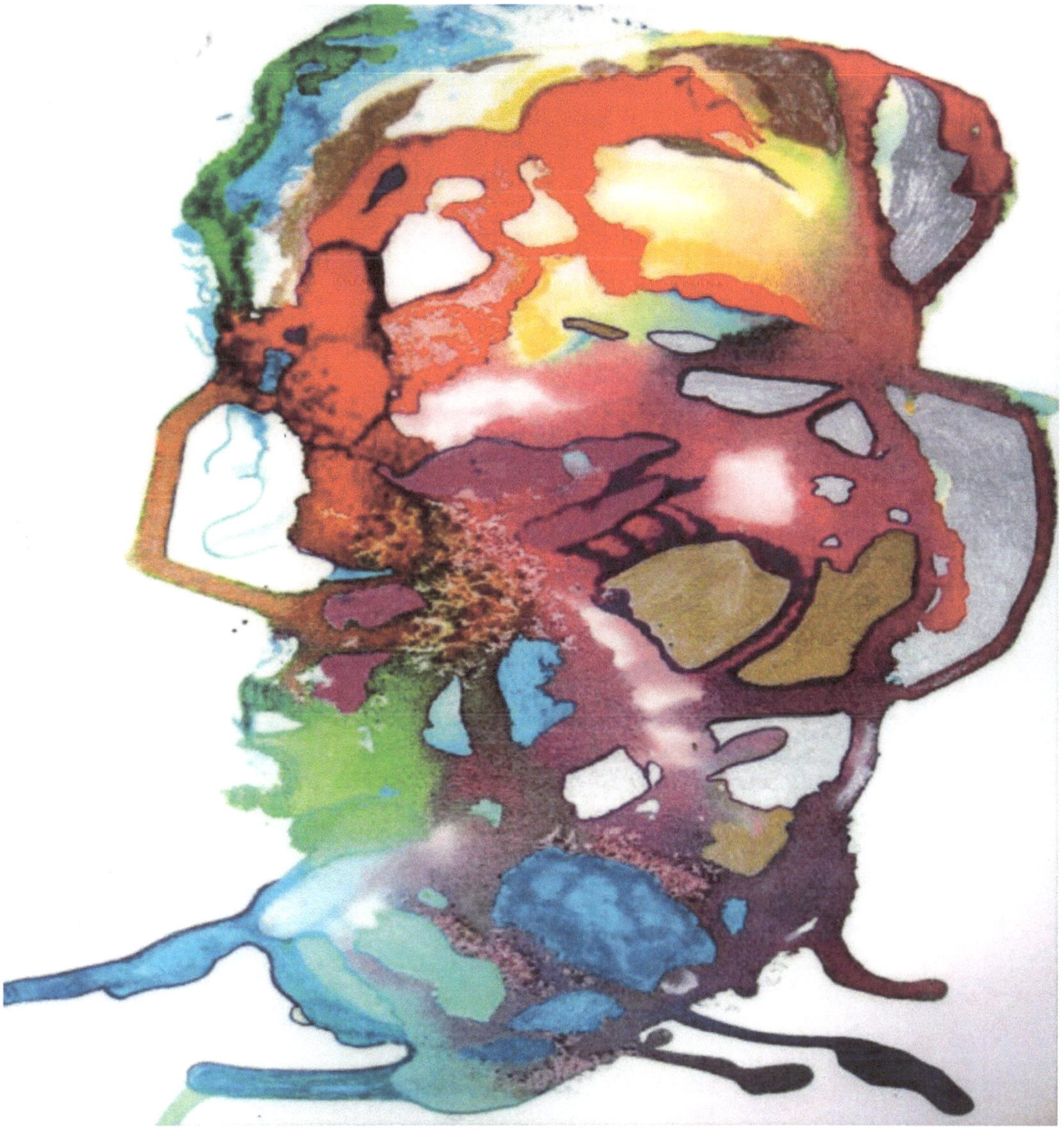

## Ronald L. Oliver

chipmunkapublishing
the mental health publisher

# A Retrospective Look:
# The Artwork of R.L. Oliver

**Front Cover:** Fire in the Belly, mixed media on canvas 2015
All text and images used are copyrighted works of Ronald L. Oliver

All rights reserved, no part of this publication may be reproduced by any means, electronic, mechanical photocopying, documentary, film or any other format without prior written permission of the publisher.

Published by
Chipmunka publishing
United Kingdom

http://www.chipmunkapublishing.com

Copyright © Ron L Oliver

ISBN 978-1-78382-5608-8

# Table of Contents

| | | | |
|---|---|---|---|
| I. | Title | ---------------------------------- | 1 |
| II. | Table of Contents | ---------------------------------- | 4 |
| III. | Introduction | ---------------------------------- | 6 |
| IV. | Early Works | ---------------------------------- | 7 |

1. Walker´s Girl ---------------------------------- 7
2. Country Doctor ---------------------------------- 8
3. James Baldwin ---------------------------------- 9
4. Jimi Hendrix ---------------------------------- 10
5. Abe ---------------------------------- 11
6. A Neighbour ---------------------------------- 12
7. Self Portrait ---------------------------------- 13
8. Moon Over Melissa ---------------------------------- 14
9. Man and Dog ---------------------------------- 14
10. Self Portrait II ---------------------------------- 16
11. Young Cowboys ---------------------------------- 18
12. Little Miss Music ---------------------------------- 19
13. Holding Tight ---------------------------------- 20
14. Melissa 1989 ---------------------------------- 21
15. After Vermeer ---------------------------------- 22
16. Yellowstone on Fire ---------------------------------- 23
17. Walking into Darkness ---------------------------------- 24
18. Grandfather Winston ---------------------------------- 25
19. Nellie Wave Waltermeyer ---------------------------------- 26
20. Big Grins ---------------------------------- 27
21. Still Life with Limes ---------------------------------- 28
22. Madonna and Child ---------------------------------- 29
23. Smell This ---------------------------------- 30
24. The Child in the Basement ---------------------------------- 31
25. The Searcher ---------------------------------- 32
26. Colorado ---------------------------------- 33
27. A Cabin in the Pines ---------------------------------- 34
28. Abstract #161 ---------------------------------- 35
29. Drawing Mother ---------------------------------- 36
30. Yellow Maraca ---------------------------------- 37
31. Flor Bromelia ---------------------------------- 38
32. Let´s Go Fly a Kite ---------------------------------- 39
33. Colombian Girl in Yumbo ---------------------------------- 40
34. The Crying Campesino ---------------------------------- 41
35. Displaced ---------------------------------- 42

| | | |
|---|---|---|
| 36. El Silletero Feliz | | 43 |
| 37. The Washerwoman | | 44 |
| 38. Jessica III | | 45 |
| 39. Secretarial | | 46 |
| 40. Shorely a Penguin | | 47 |
| V. Later Works | | 48 |
|   A. Cockleburs | | 49 |
|   B. Rainbow Sprouts | | 50 |
|   C. Rooted in Randomness | | 51 |
|   D. Rooted in Whimsy | | 52 |
|   E. Fire in the Belly | | 53 |
|   F. Crayon Jungle | | 54 |
|   G. Flaming Bananas | | 55 |
|   H. Cerebral Roots | | 56 |
|   I. Disintegration | | 57 |
|   J. Primordial Growth | | 58 |
|   K. Dissolving World | | 59 |
|   L. A Rock Just Told | | 60 |
|   M. Pensando en Agua | | 61 |
|   N. Cafetero | | 62 |
|   O. Quechuan Aguatero | | 63 |
| VI. Recent Works | | 64 |
|   Alone Again, Naturally | | 64 |
|   Girl from the Philippines | | 65 |
|   Watermelon Shade | | 66 |
|   The Golden Rubber Tree | | 67 |

**Appendix A**
**List of Illustrations**      68

# Introduction

This collection looks back at the drawings and paintings done over a lifetime. It began with a hunger to create by drawing when I was around twelve years old. This book represents a chance to put them altogether into a whole that may make more sense.

From the start, I have used drawing and painting as a way of calming down, concentrating and focusing on settling things around me. By calling them "artwork" I could make them look as I wanted them to remain. I thought they should speak with my voice and say what I wanted to say. It came natural to me because that was what I wanted. It was just that simple. I still see things that way: there is the passing and there is the fixed. It seems like there was a basic need to draw, paint, and express what was inside. I could organize and put things together on paper or canvas that went together in no other way, at no other time. It was a way out of myself and I took it. At times, it was the best way to do things when was no other way.

I was first inspired by a glossy photo-journal of the early sixties with photographs of Caroline Kennedy on top of a horse. They went together and it all made sense. Her father was highly esteemed but was later shot while riding a convertible in Dallas, but Caroline lives. It makes for a sad story but that is the way that many stories go. One lives and learns.

When I later tried to ride a horse in imitation it ran to the middle of an interstate expressway and stopped in its tracks. I loved horses until I learned they were not all without fault. I found they had a will of their own that was often greater than that of the rider. Regardless, they were often better on paper than in real life. I started drawing with a pencil and charcoal but later graduated to oils paints, acrylics, pastels and finally watercolours. I saved the best for last.

I still search for a permanent beauty, a harmony that may not be there otherwise, and a deep satisfaction when it comes out as I wanted it in the first place. It helps me to keep me away from feeling scattered and pointless, disorganized. Art was good therapy then and is good therapy now. The process still works. I would encourage anyone with the smallest well of desire or need to jump in the water, to get wet. It feels good, and the water is fine.

Over the years, I have found that my pursuit of creating comes only in bursts and spells. There were times when I felt moved to do it. There were times when I had no desire at all. The desire, the passion usually happened only once or twice a year. At times, a drought would come when I mostly twiddled my thumbs and carried on. I never found a way to pursue this interest in the everyday world. Everyone knew that artists starved. Who wants to pursue a trail to starvation?

I think this unfortunate state needs to change. The older I grew the greater was the desire to do images of people and things that mattered most. I think we are all drawn to what is most important in our lives. I hope you are ready to join me in looking back over sixty years of life in service to others in small towns, small cities and finally big cities. I hope you find it enjoyable.

I: Early Works

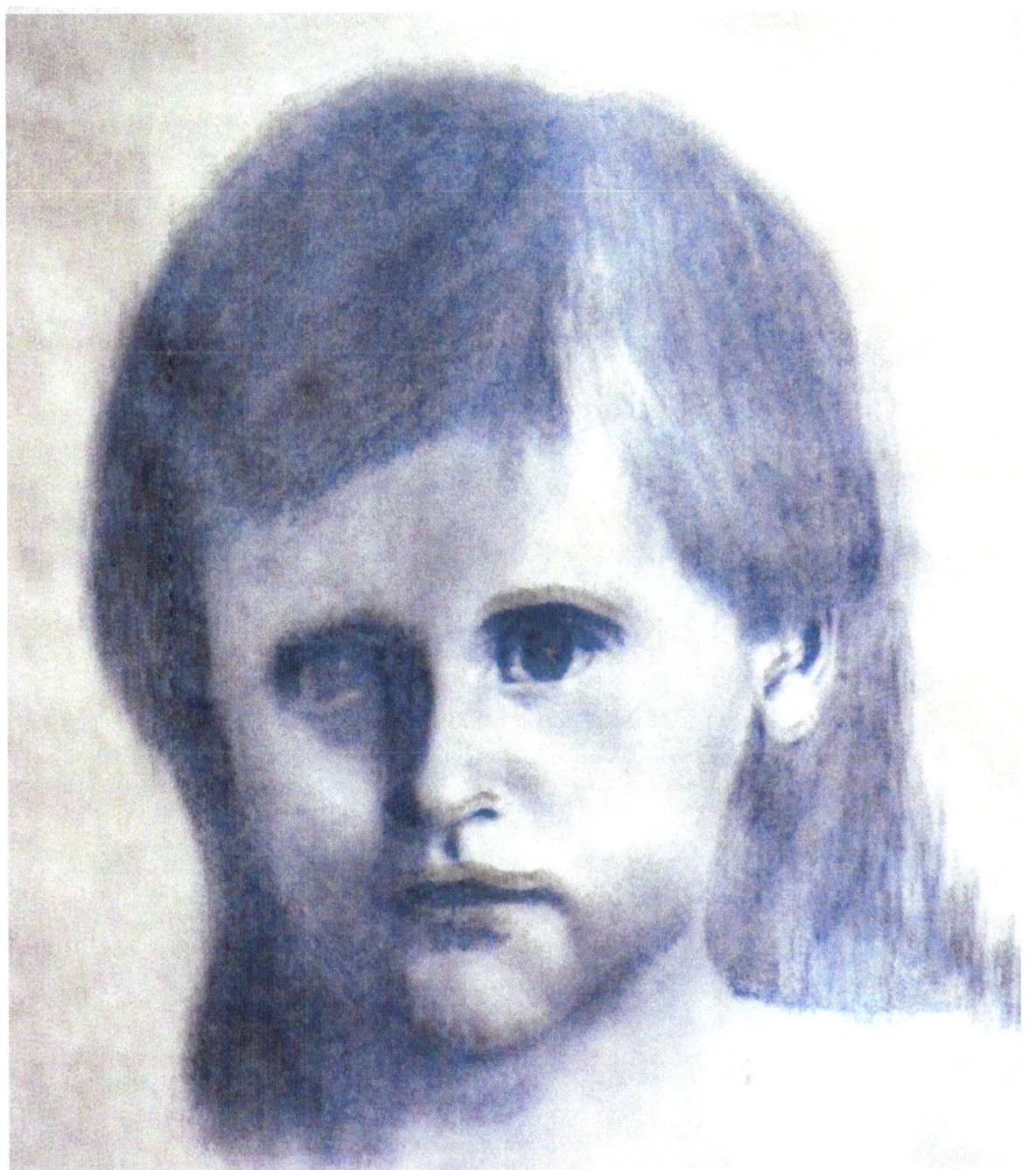

**Walker's Girl**

I remember first drawing this with a new set of artist pencils embossed with numbered Hs and Gs that I knew nothing about. I later added to this trove with sticks of charcoal that came in transparent plastic and placed them all on the "melmac" kitchen table to draw. My biggest fear was making a hole in the paper. The fear was of making a big mistake that would result in endless erasing to minimize or escape it. My first attempts had left paper with holes in it, so, I remember this doing this drawing with as much care as I knew how to give. I worked carefully to do it repeated coats and layers of graphite.

In the end, I discovered that one eye came out darker than the other. I found it fascinating that the drawing still reached out at you despite the seeming defect. I found that sometimes the defect attracted the needed second look. Now, am not sure if this contrast was done with intention or not. I only knew that I first saw her face first after my brother gave me a copy of **Let Us Now Praise Famous Men**. It was a classic work from 1941 done by Walker Evans and James Agee classic from the days of the Dust Bowl and Great Depression. People like this little girl got left behind as it particularly hard on farmers and their families in the South. I think the girl was from Alabama and was an offspring of the sharecroppers, a people still widely despised. I always had a lot of sympathy for them and the little girl standing on the porch looking straight at you could not be side stepped. It was if she wanted to say ¨Yep, you´re another peeping Tom… another looker, someone that´s just going to stand there and gawk at me like I am helpless and need pity.¨ She was right. I stood there and gawked at her. I wanted to see it all and get a close look at her. Her face was and is haunting.

I wanted to understand suffering, but without making major mistakes. I knew the girl had something to say about living with want and how to best do it. This drawing has been with for nearly fifty years. I have carried it from city to city and hung it proudly on my office wall for years. I wanted to keep a reminder around. Now the image of the little girl feels like it is part of me.

**Country Doctor** 1969

I remember seeing this image on an ad for a John Houston movie that told about 18$^{th}$ or 19$^{th}$ century Ireland. All cast members had sensitive faces. I guess it was largely about how to confront a barren life with dignitary. That did not mean winning big or becoming the king on the hill but simple knuckling under and doing what was needed. The country doctor did just that in leading role that led to dignity of self and others, though I have long since forgotten the story and the details.

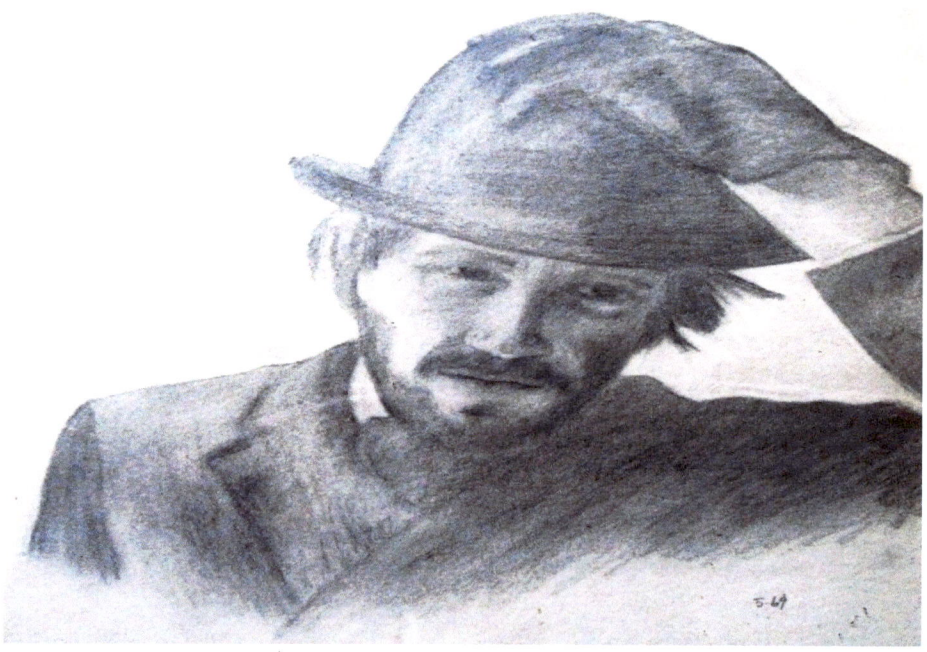

## James Baldwin

The image I drew made it look like he was fresh from a pounding and still had the shiner to prove it. Otherwise, there is not much to say about this warrior except he lived during hard times. He was much like my brother. At times, he exploded. Mr. Baldwin had a reputation for exploding with passion that staked out clear limits to his tolerance. He gave new meaning to being hot under the collar, or so that was how my brother told the story. Fighters of injustice, it seems, must have a core of passion that keeps fighting and will not take part in injustice, come rain or shine. I knew injustice was common and it still happened which means that fighters need to know how to weather the storm, how to take a punch. I knew it happened all the time.

In the late fifties and early sixties protest marches were rampant in the city and had been for several years. The young were leading the way to fair treatment. At that time, my brother was a student and reporter for the university newspaper. He attended all protest gatherings that he could get to or find a way to mornings or nights. I can remember him going off to a protest march in his pajama top thinking he was ready to witness history. He really did not care how he looked when he was out to serve justice. I try to minimize exterior, meaningless things, too.

James Baldwin was a writer's writer, an intellectual's intellectual. He chose to live abroad for years. He found that he could not stomach the stark injustice over the long run, either. Not being able to stomach your home is a sad thing, but he left a testimony, and he did make a difference. He saw in his imagination the cities of America burn before they burned. There were many storms and many fires in the drive for civil rights. You only had to read the book or listen to the words he spoke **The Fire Next Time** to know that he was speaking the truth as he knew it. My hat is off to him. He wrote with power and a fierce will. Sorrow so often plays on such a flat, featureless field.

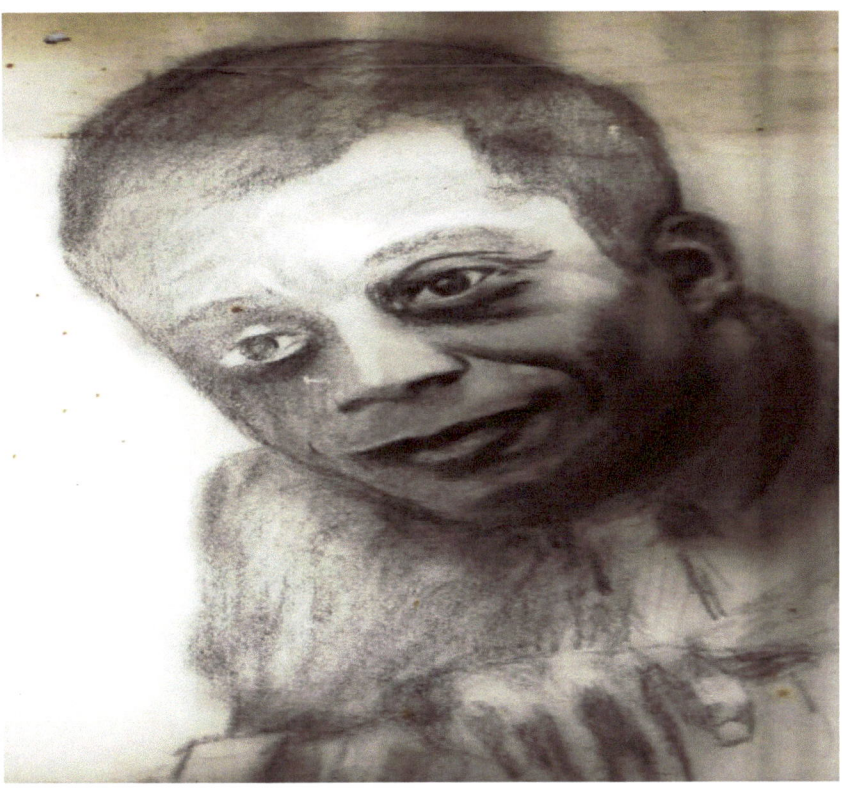

## Jimi Hendrix

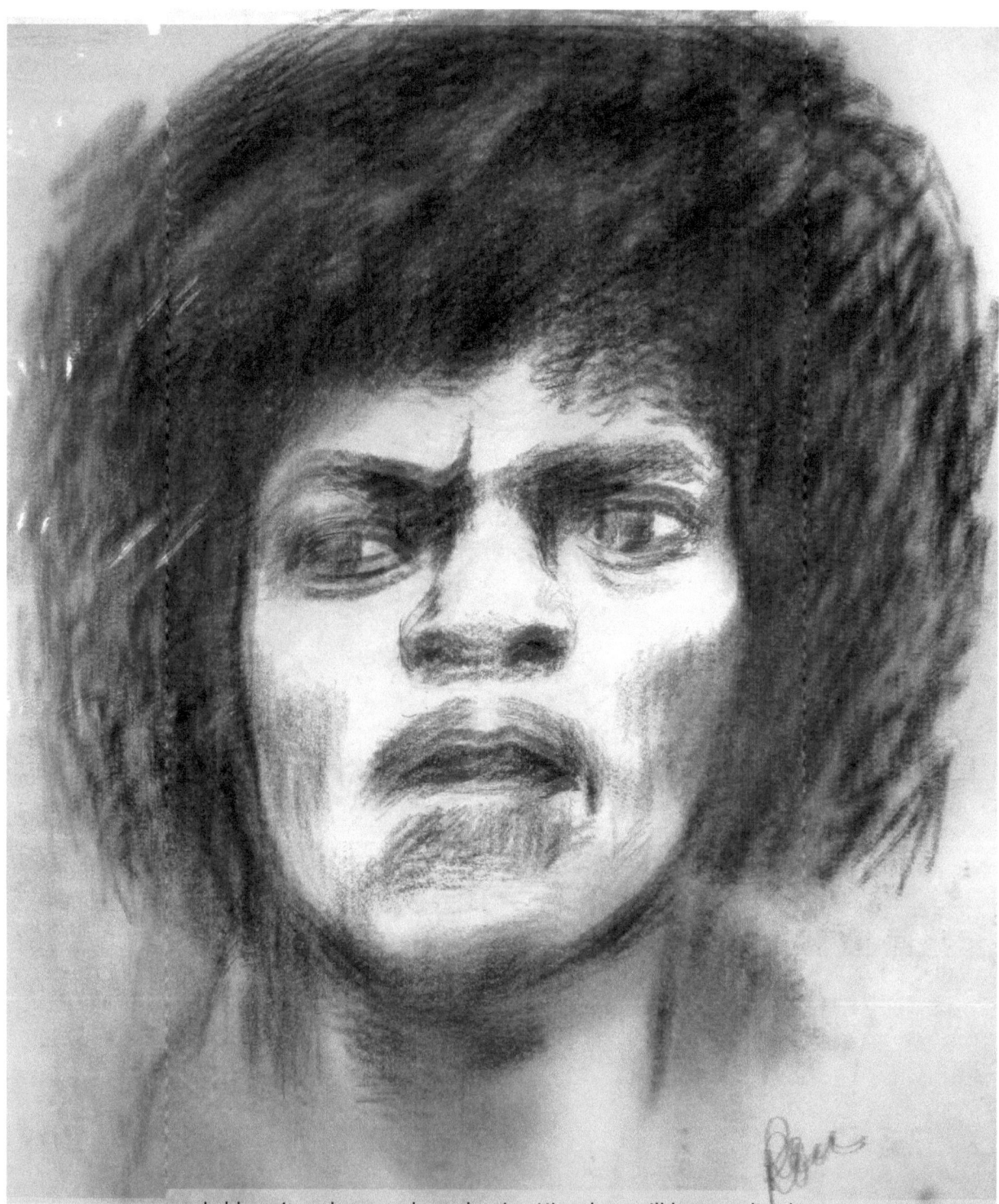

He was such a remarkable guitar player and vocal artist. His talent will long outlive him, and he will not be soon forgotten. He played guitar with unmistakable skill and with a flow that was remarkable. Most people also knew that he was going to crash and burn if he was not lucky. He was lucky enough.

## Abe

Abe was born after I graduated from college and began a career in social work. I remember well the cold weather: blowing snow and ice on the streets to the hospital. I drew this with charcoal in 1976, soon after leaving Oklahoma City and after showing my early works in the first Starving Artist Exhibition at the Fair Grounds.

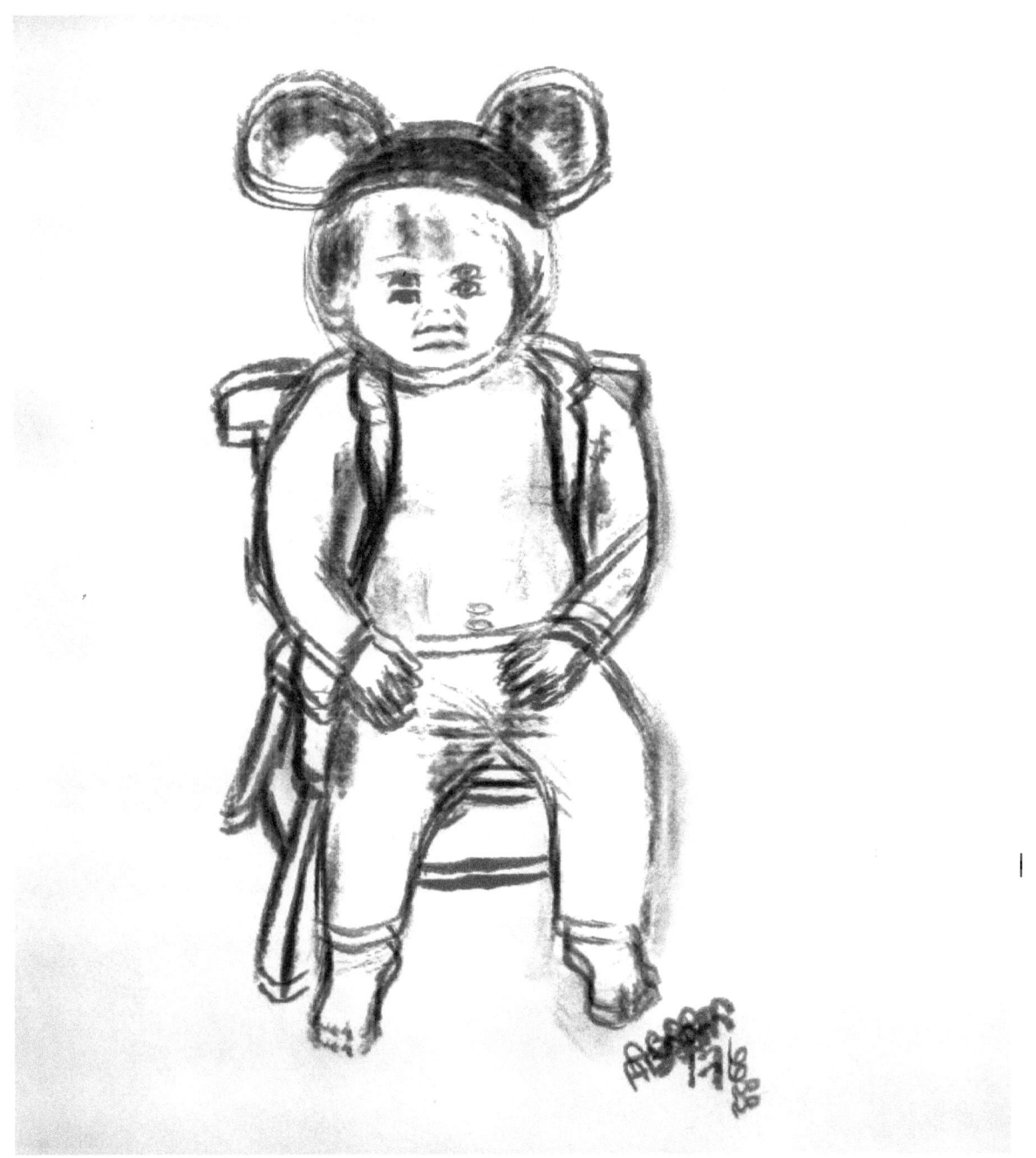

**A Neighbour - 1976**

This is one of my less remembered drawings of a neighbour girl that had a most determined look. I remember mostly being captivated by the dark flowing hair and its swirls of black. What was most clear was the determination and certainty of the expression on her face. I tried to show it, and it came out well, I think. The look was almost hammer-like in intensity and I have always admired that kind of courage and hammered determination. This girl seemed to have both.

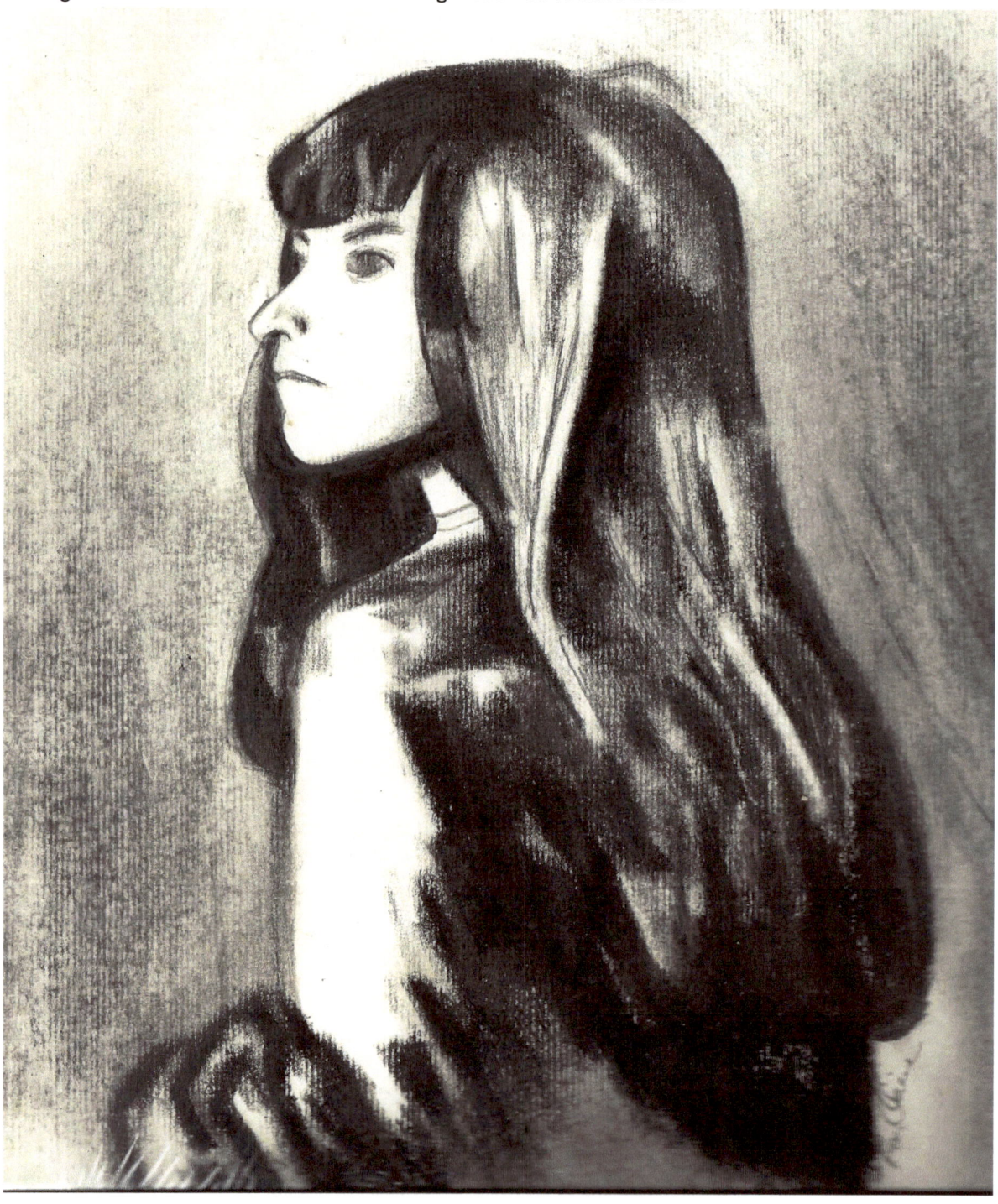

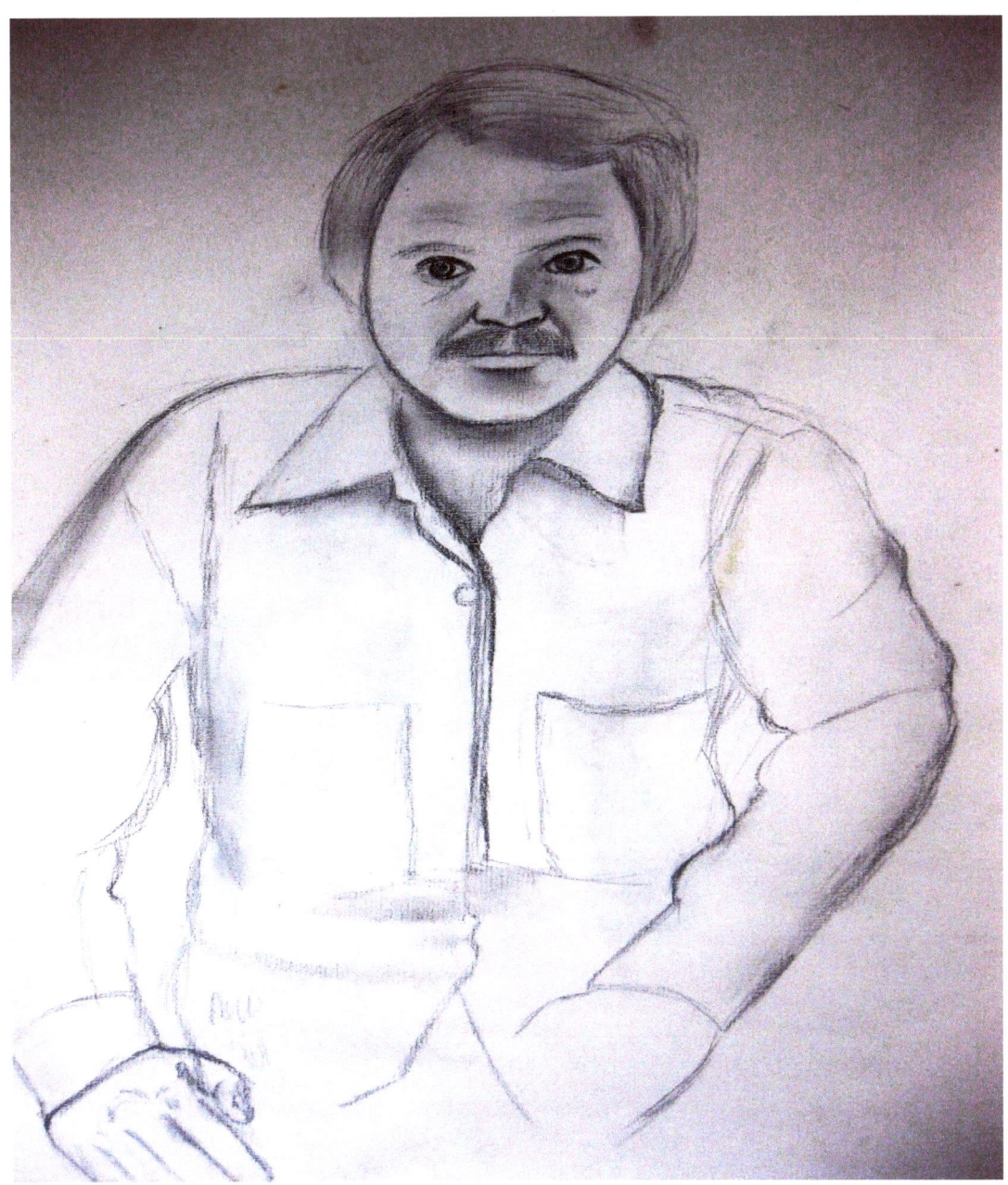

**Self Portrait 1978**

My career was getting underway and I had bought an acacia-speckled house on the edge of town. Life was looking up since moving across the street from a large plant nursery and loving to have it where it belonged and was needed. Also, I remember doing a yellow and brown mural on the dining room wall that had a large encircling tree that brought people together, it seemed. There was a clear warmth to it that used brightness and boldness with a daffodil yellow.

Unfortunately, I have no record of the mural and no photograph. Instead I offer this graphite self-portrait done with quick simple lines. The sun was coming out and I wanted to save the thought.

## Moon Over Melissa

Talking aloud about former loves and ecstasies is not easy. Instead, I will just say that I think this charcoal drawing done in 1981. I added some ink and charcoal and thought I had nearly captured the essence of this lady. At least it is as good as any drawing I have collected. Yes, she was beautiful.

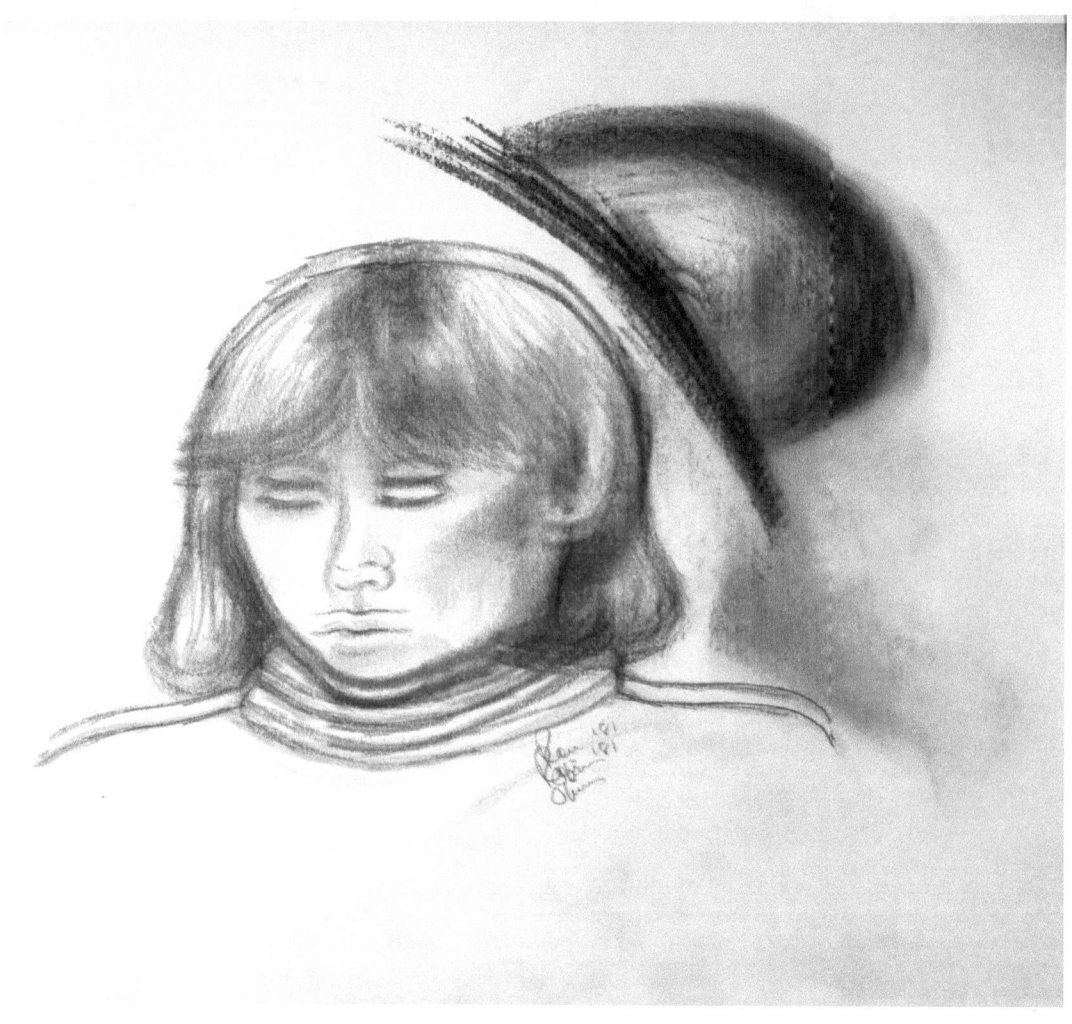

## Man and Dog

Also known as The Tramp on the Street

He looks like such a deserving beggar, doesn't he? He looked so to me or so it seemed. I have interpreted this drawing in several ways over the years: as a testament of need and destitution with a kind heart, as an illustration of a bereft man and dog, as a testament to the love between man and animal, even as a roundabout reworking of Jethro Tull album cover image, which it was.

Speaking of which, I saw the musical group called Jethro Tull when they performed in Tulsa in the late sixties. I loved their music. It had so many peaks and valleys and the leader wielded his instrument with such poise and assuredness. The playing was done with conviction and he played as though he was floating on the music. Such a talent! It was such fun to watch his mastery.

The band had nothing but gifted musicians with a leader that inspired awe so readily, so easily. He created his own world with the music and stayed there until it ended. I wondered at the time whether he felt at all like he was swimming in music? For the audience, there were no doubt many fellow swimmers. I wondered if they saw the auditorium as an airport. It might have felt like heaven to them, they seemed to enjoy it so much. I wondered if they were a flight path of their own making and simply soaring. Trying to capture the forlorn with the joyful was what I wanted to show. I wanted to put all these feelings together as a way of complimenting their work.

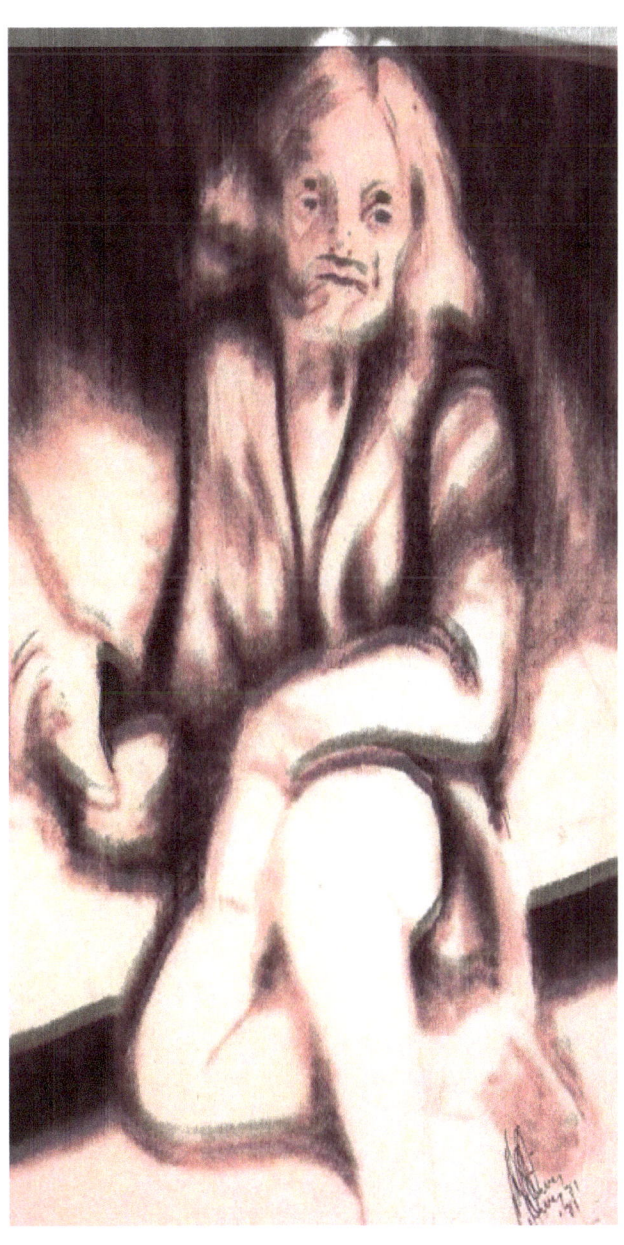

**Self-Portrait February 1982**

I had my beard grown from about this time. At first It worried me some. I did not want to come across as being too ¨out there¨, as if my feet didn´t touch ground. I lived in a very conservative part of Oklahoma at the time and tolerance of weirdos was slim and none. . Maybe weird cowboys could get away with more of the outrageous, but community folk needed to show up for work clean shaven or with at most a moustache. That made for a clearer identity it seemed.

At that time, I was making a new home and looking for acceptance, even though I came from ¨the North. ¨ Yes, I did. I was from Tulsa, Northern Oklahoma. I worked in what was known then as ¨Little Dixie¨. We were known for having farthest west standing confederate statue on our courthouse lawn. The farthest west confederate statute was in Sherman, Texas. Sherman and Denison, the childhood home of Dwight Eisenhower, were nearby.

I was slow in speech, even took pride in slow speech as well as relishing words of affection, like sunshine, honey, and Sweetie pie! I was often among and on the side of those who spoke with honey-dripping lips. I was known as being on the side of the down and out. The gossip was that if you weren´t deprived or poverty-stricken I would give you little of my time. My background was in knowing the meaning of losing. I had attended and graduated from a second-rate regional college. But I dreamed of being first-rate. At the time, it was just a dream with me. I knew I was a Southerner, and all Southerners were losers, weren´t they? They were widely known as being losers from the top of their head to the bottom of their feet, to the souls of their shoes… if they wore any.

When I was in college, I had taken a trip to see Ole Miss and its home in Oxford, Mississippi. Specifically, I had gone with my brother, Charles, to see William Faulkner´s grave. Charles drove a black Volkswagen Beetle. It wasn´t spoken aloud but we both knew that we went there to worship at the grave of William Faulkner. This pilgrimage was done though I knew down deep that Ernest Hemingway was the better writer. Ernest Hemingway was more of a match for my simple tastes, less windy, though less eloquent and so much less cluttered when looking at his work on the page. I had read where he stood to write to spare his aching back. For some reason, that always impressed me.

Still, I remember standing there at attention and being transfixed by the eternal flame and the seeming majesty of the grave. I identified myself as a ¨new¨ Southerner, I would bask in the glow of the top of the mountain at times, but still often felt right at home in low places. I believed that all men were equal, and I believed in need for a social imperative that said all humans were equal in the way that treatment and rights were dished out. All in all, I was quite liberal and tolerant. I was proud of it. Hadn´t I protested and acted when a northside vender of childcare told me she didn´t tend to black babies and they weren´t welcome at her place of business. And, I voted for George McGovern, though he lost in his run for presidency by a wide margin. Regrets have since been noted. The flower children after all lost in both 1968 and 1972. They were not meant to rule. Some would give thanks for that. So, I just voted my thoughts and feelings in 1972, and lost. But I would do it again… thoughts and feelings are important.

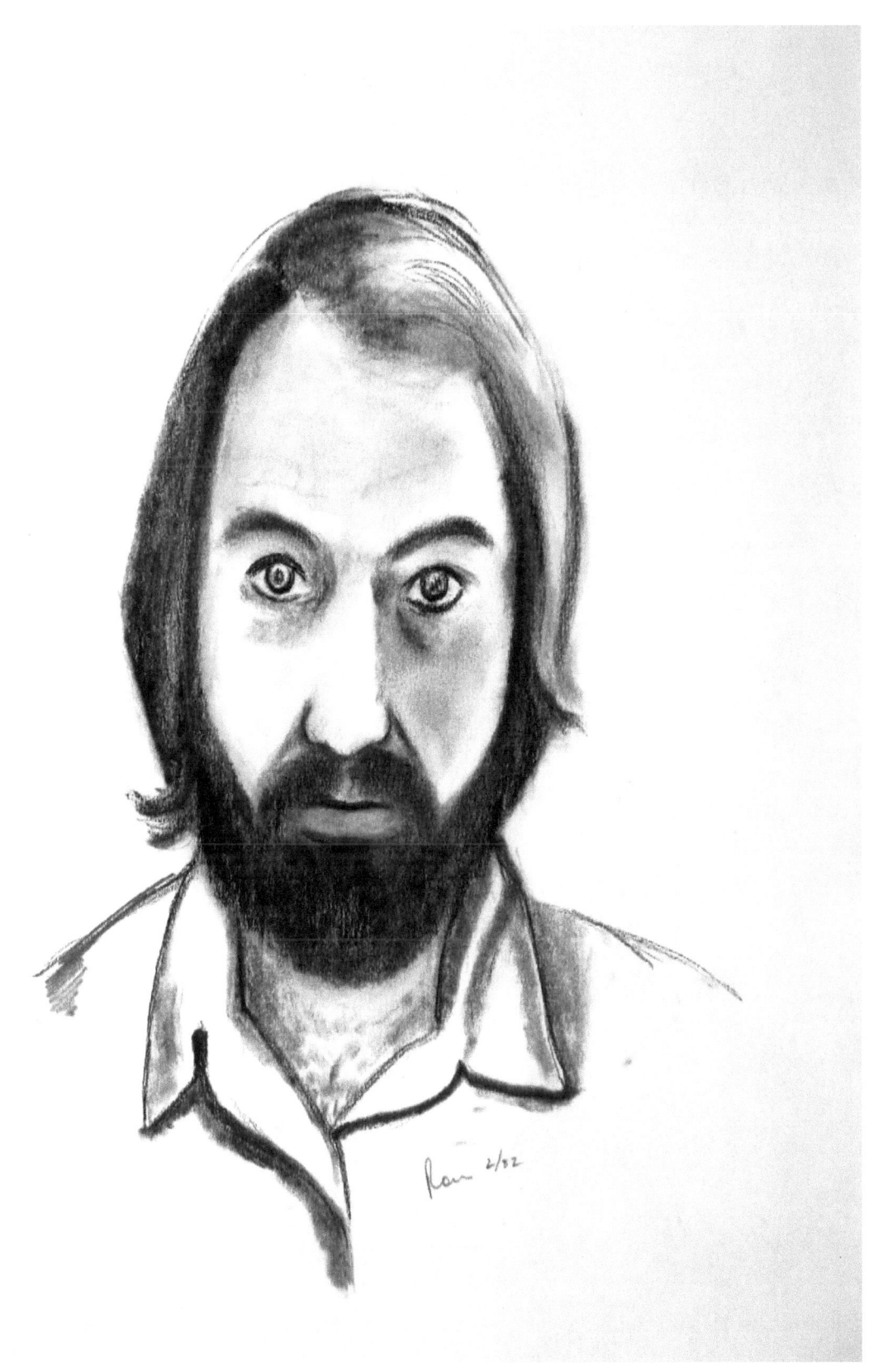

Young Cowboys - 1982

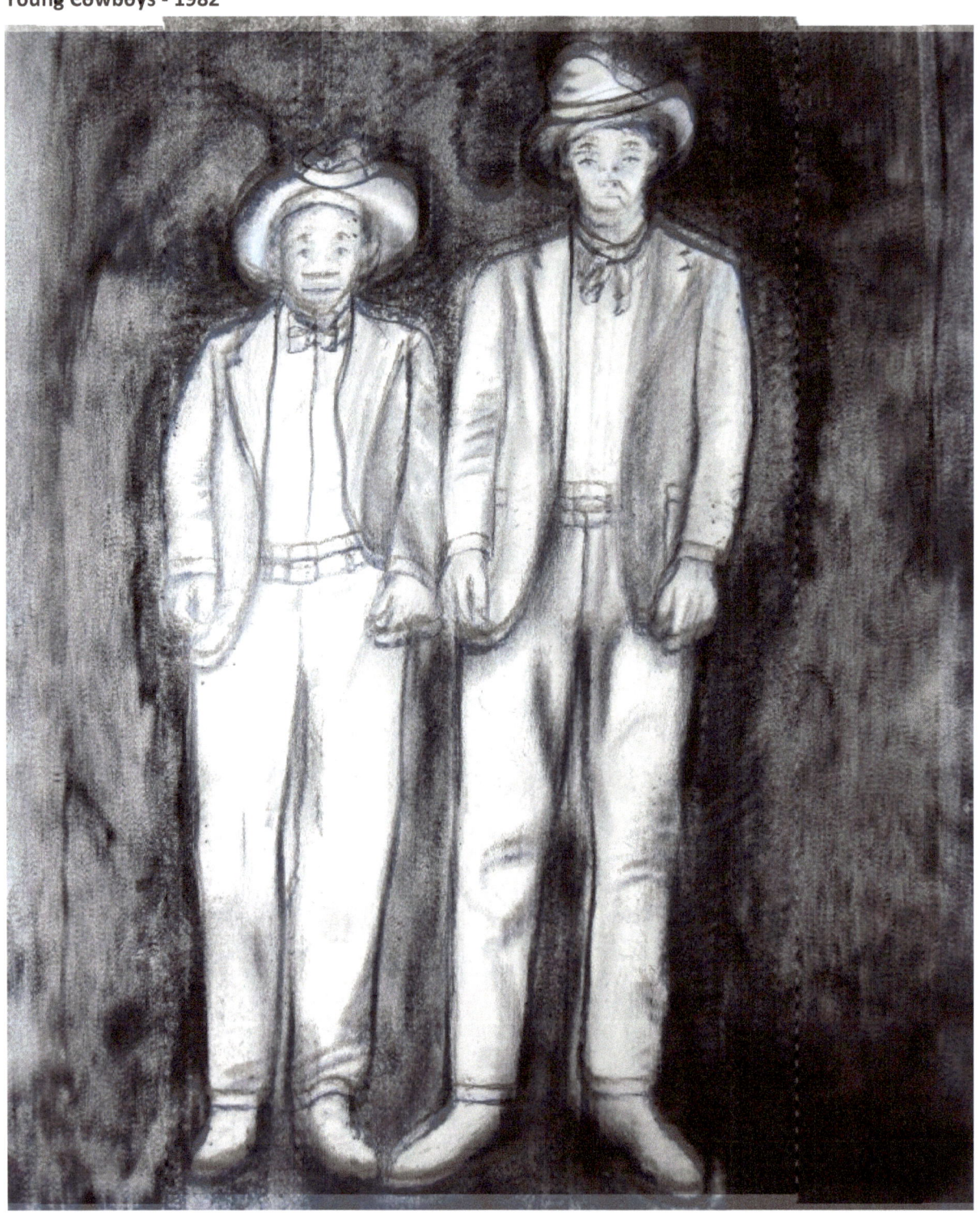

I found these two boys that I painted in ink, and charcoal and drew with pencil in a ditch near Achille, Oklahoma, just south of where I lived in Durant. A tornado had nabbed the turn-of-the-century photo and tossed it away. I was curious about the disaster but much more curious about these two good ole boys dressed up in their Sunday bests and going to town to have their picture taken... so I drew them.

# Little Miss Music c 1988

At the time I did this drawing, I was living in Vermillion, South Dakota, and teaching at the University of South Dakota. I was in my second year of teaching. I lived for three or four years in Meckling, South Dakota on the road to Yankton. Yankton was more of a hub town while Vermillion sat at the end of the line. I thought I had come to the end of the line and was parked near the end of a dead-end street. Little did I know how the future would unfold. It was over before I knew it. While it was a time to learn to play acoustic guitar in a group, it was not otherwise rewarding. Soon, too soon, I thought, it was over and I moved on.

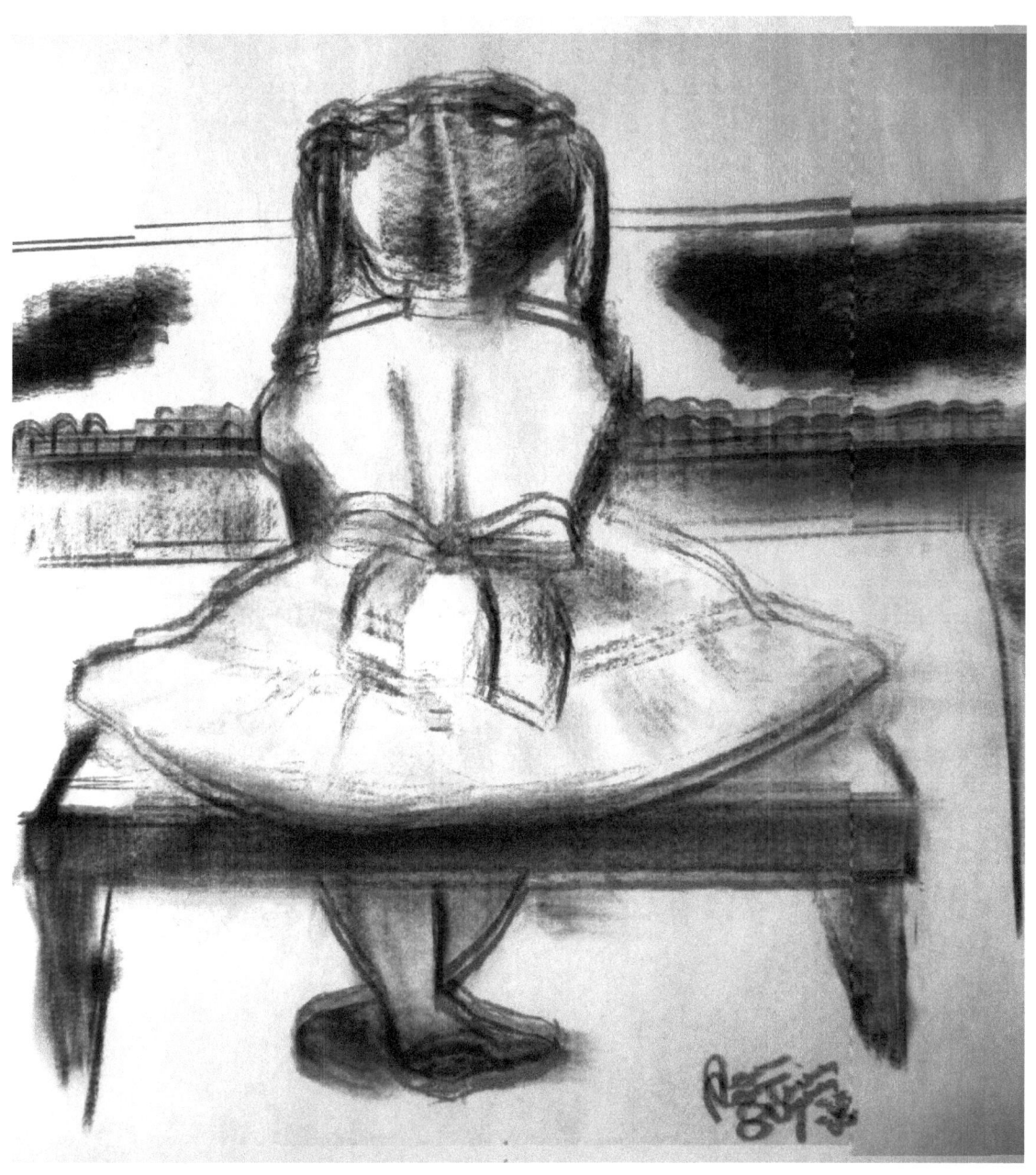

**Holding Tight 1989**

The source of this image? I do not recall. At the time I only knew it touched me with its warmth. The Big Hands of a Big Sister could be the subtitle. I have also thought that it shows what a Big Sister can do and be. I had a big sister, so I thought I knew much about authority and sibling love based mostly on sibling birth order, as known as Adlerian psychology. But I only had one sister, so did I know that much about it?

I had found in my study of family counseling that Alfred Adler spoke often of this dynamic. They said he was a mile deep, but I never dug that far to know. While Freud thought we were best conceptualized as unitary beings that responded to seasons, Adler knew we were paired with others from beginning to end. We all had ¨social interest¨ and we all lived in networked connected by the roots and sharing our roots as family systems.

I had the good fortune to hear a descendant of Adler speak at length in Seattle. As I recall, he was as much convinced that he needed an obsessive accountant to keep his records as he was sure that we were all psychologically turned toward one another. That idea went together with being the in the arms of a Big Sister. I always thought it would make a fine illustration.

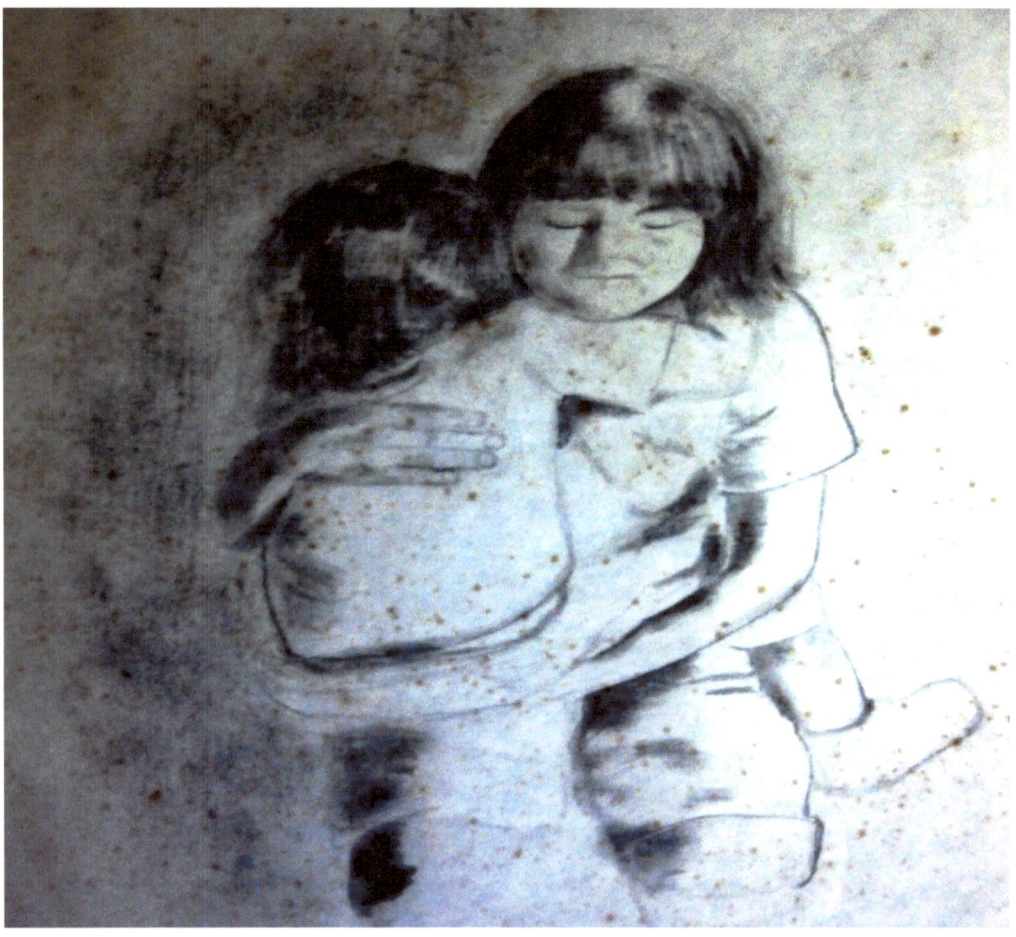

**Melissa - 1989**

A drawing done with pencil and charcoal to a woman that fascinated me in every way possible. I thought sometimes she had been born only to fascinate men and that it was no challenge for her, it came so easy. What I am trying to say is that I thought Melissa was beautiful.

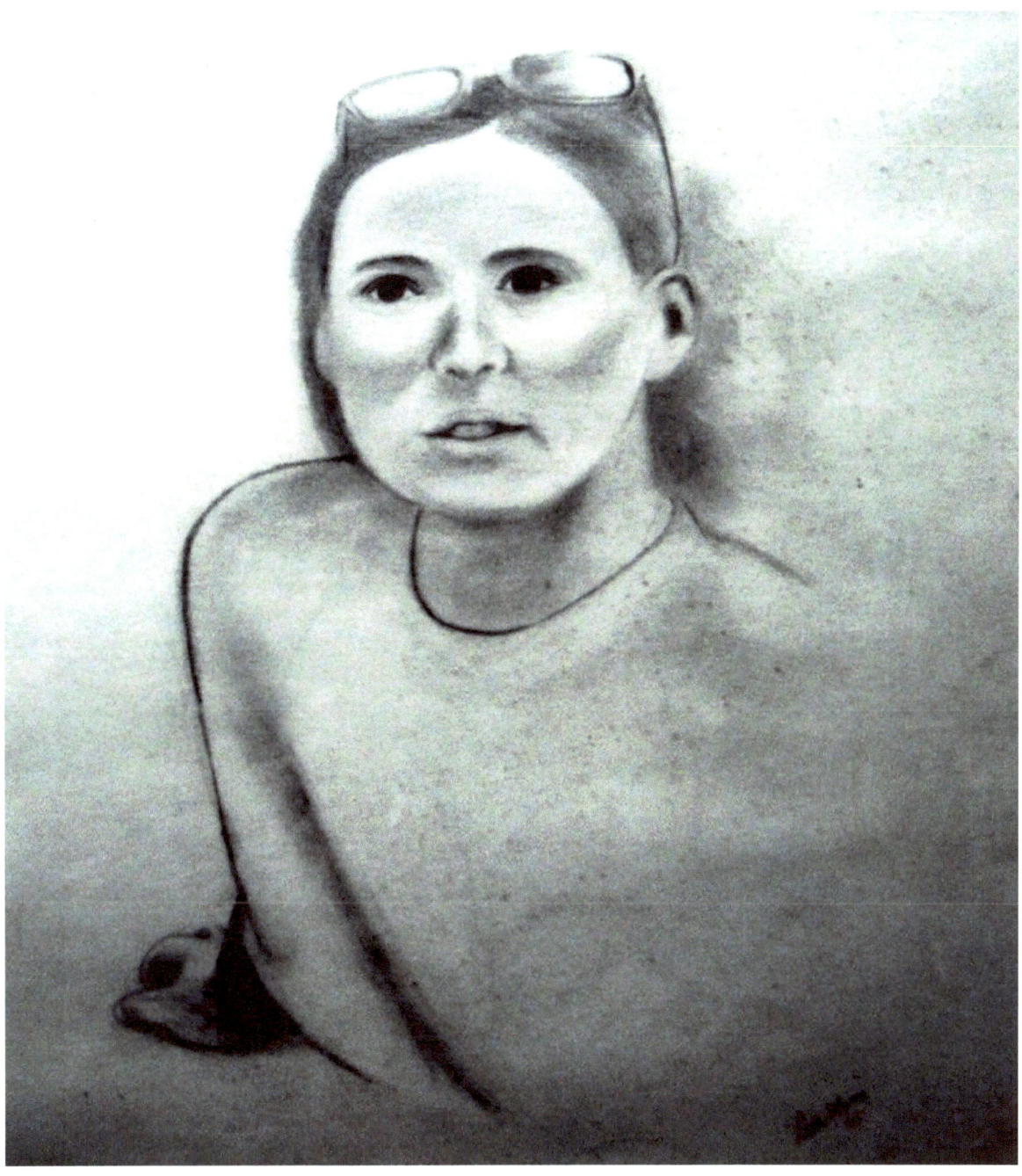

## After Vermeer

Honestly, you will not get an unbiased account from me as to the exquisite abilities of Jan Vermeer: **The Girl with a Pearl Earring**, 1655, is still the standard-bearer for perfection in form, color and tone. I have read that he knew the fundamentals of light and photography in the 17th century. If so, this is not an artist to discuss with any sort of supposed objectivity. To me he breathed perfection.

This image used acrylic paint and imagination. I tried to fashion a figure with a predominant hat could be featured as it was most appealing. This image has that look of having just arrived at the port of call. I saw the sea in the sky and the threads of beads as strings of jute and the lightest of cottons. When I did this painting, I had been divorced for three or four years and wanted to paint what was out there to see. I still relish the image.

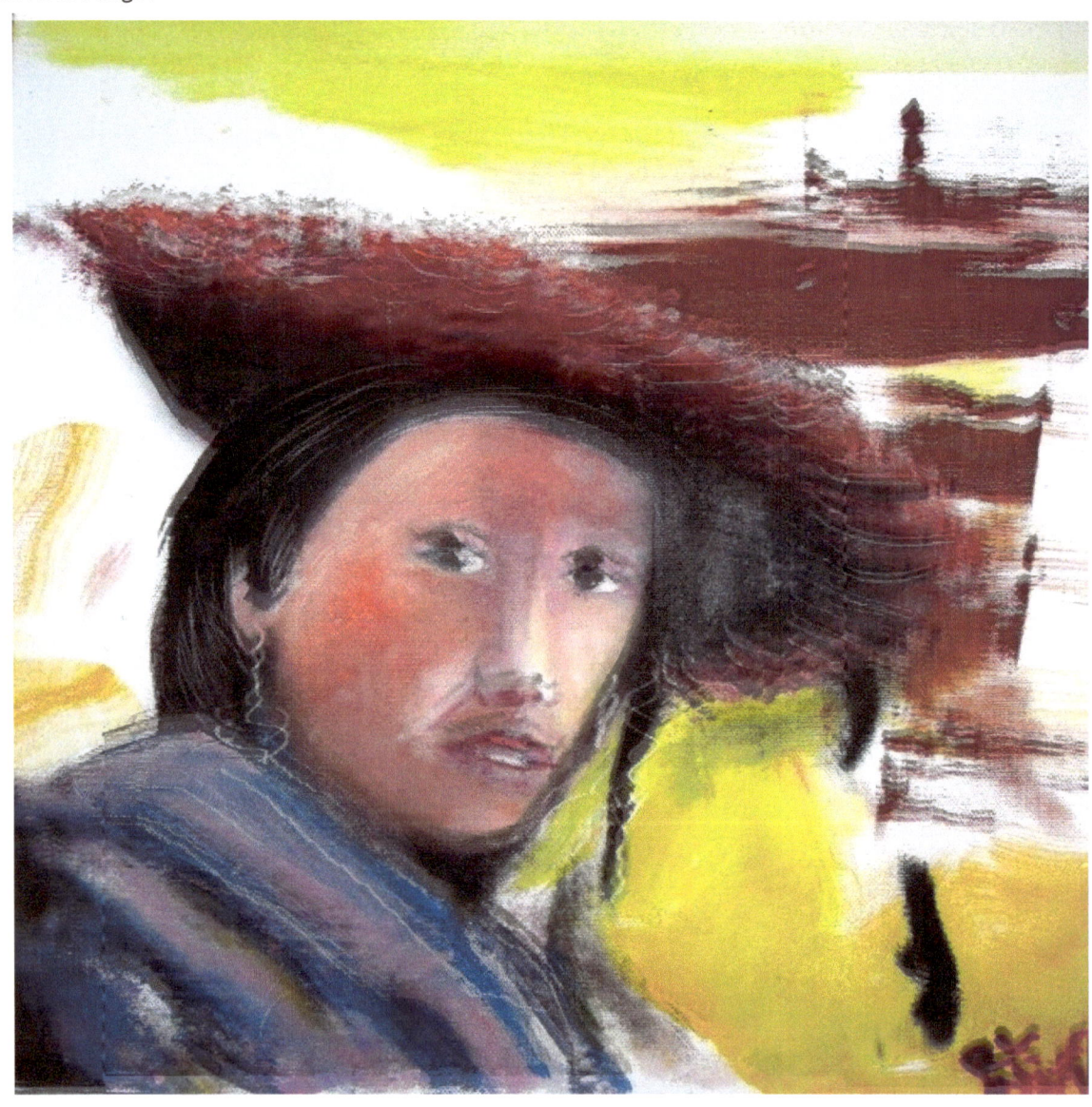

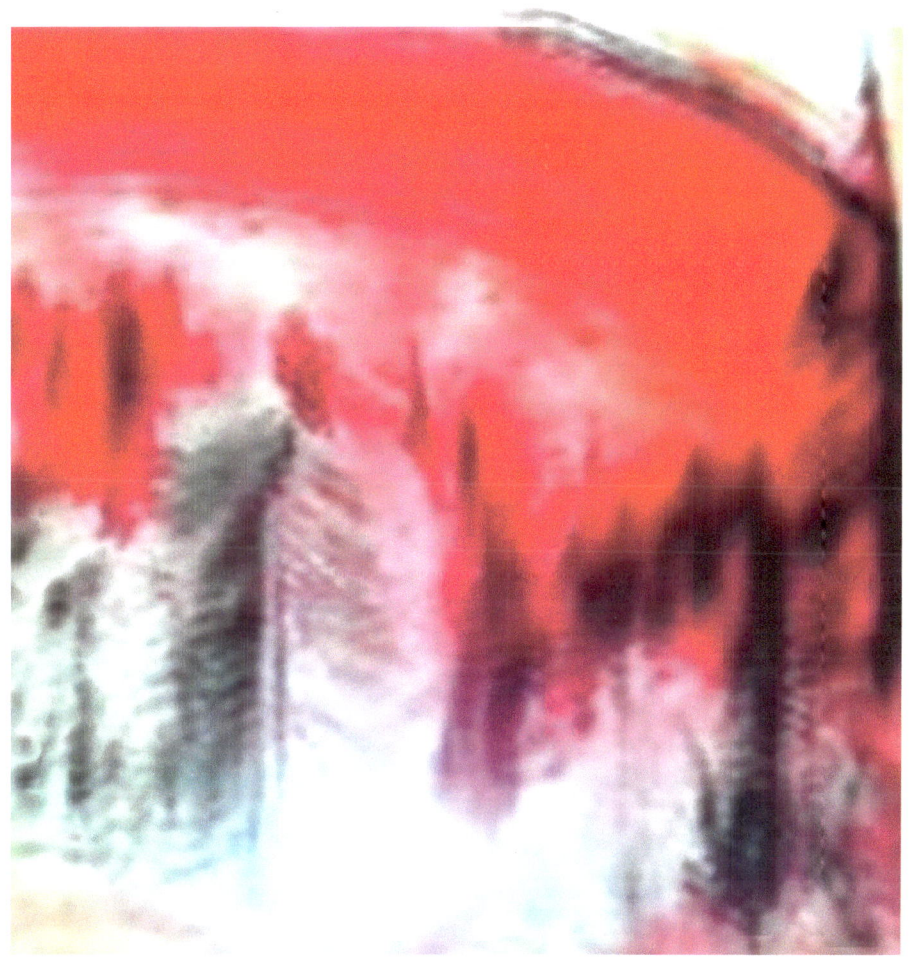

## Yellowstone on Fire

This work was done with dry pastels on paper. I think it was my first adventure into solitary bright, flaming colors and the color I emphasized was red. I saw red until there was nothing aside of the flaming red. This was seen after two trips to Yellowstone Park. The first trip was green and yellow and terra cotta all monumental in size and breath-taking in beauty. The first time I saw the green beauty on a trip during the summer of about 1987 and the second time was 1989. Instead of mainly green, the second trip was right after the large fire in the park that blackened nearly everything. The second trip was sad black, and it was one of the saddest, most forsaken scenes I have ever seen. Black just can't be used to cover over or tidy-up green. It did not work then it does not work now.

## Walking into Darkness 1991

In my last year at the University South Dakota I was plumbing the increasing depths of psychology. These were the days of narrative therapy, when you could explore telling a "therapeutic" story. The Social Worker, Lee Wallas, told her **Stories That Heal**. The one about walking backwards like a crab was told to a young boy that did everything backwards and she witnessed his psychological rebirth. It was a hopeful, promising time. But it was also a time of political correctness, e.g. hyperbole was increasingly taboo and "unscientific" in every way. Science seemed to increasingly distance itself from art. It was as if a cosmic question had been asked: Who wants more than the simplest and direct expression?

Science overshadowed art and at times seemed to look for its elimination. I pretended that there was no conflict and went on drawing images of the therapy that I believed in. One example is this is the work called ¨Walking into Darkness¨. It was a runny and stained process but that I assumed to be vital if you wanted to avoid walking while wounded. We all find a way to do it, my hunch is.

As once said ¨It was the best of time. And, it was the worst of time¨. I remember it now as a time of hurdles. One had to watch what one said if one wished to remain academically attuned. There was widespread protest being heard about returning to pure science and just forgetting about this so-called psychobabble. It was increasingly seen as not offering anything concrete, anything sensible, anything usable and repeatable. In fact, the last part of the decade was overflowing with meta studies that brought the whole field into question. They were looking for the validity of the field of psychiatry and did not find it. Instead, it was found that there was no difference between a pill and a person, also known as a Psychiatrist. There was no validity data to show that a designated professional could do anything more than a pill could do. They were sobering times.

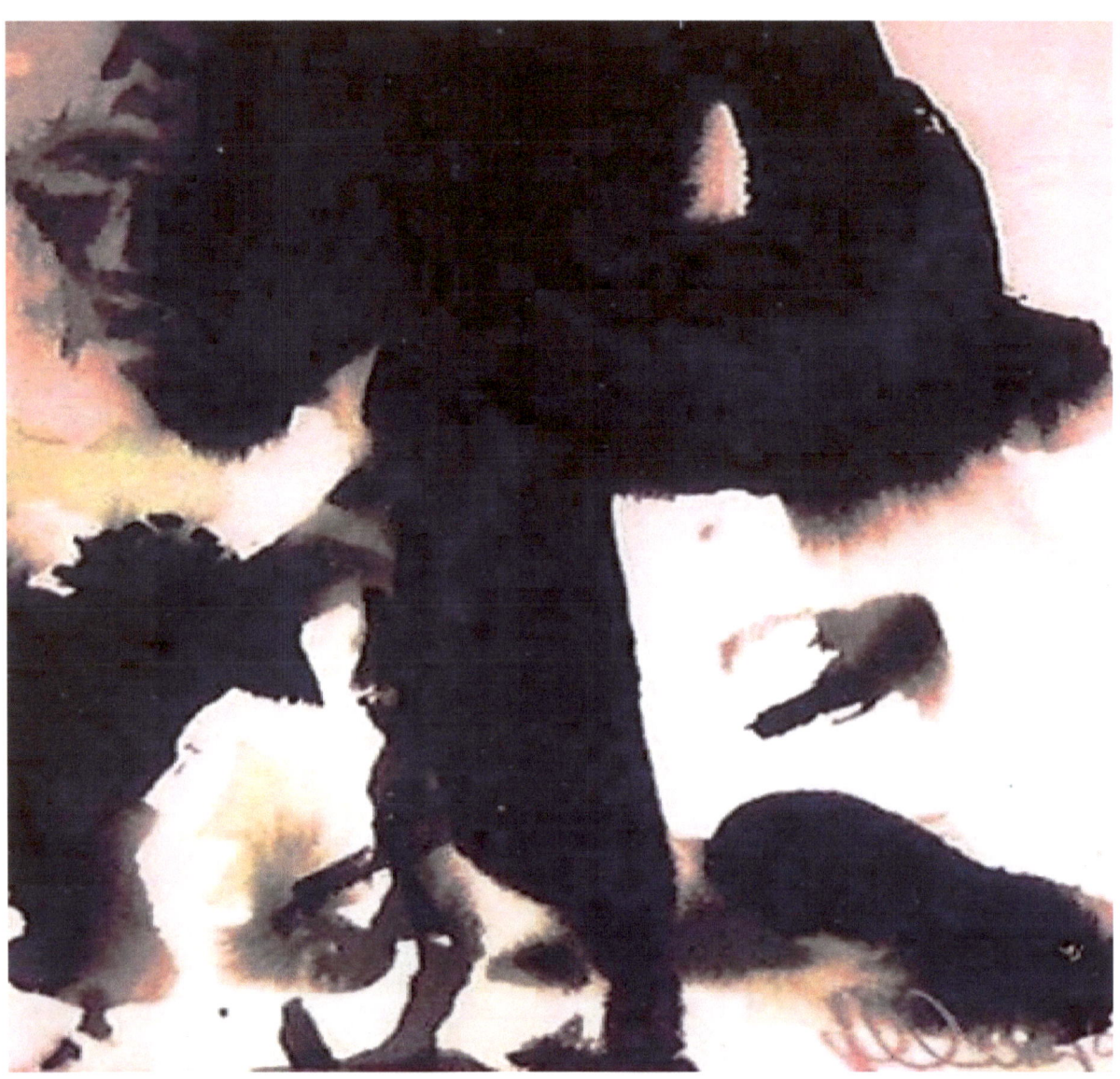

Later, in 2008, I used this image for a book cover for **Flight from Colombia**. It was not well received as a fictional work.  In fact, I was told that it lacked any sense of character development.  Maybe that is what happens when a fictional character doesn´t grow. Maybe they did not want to grow up, nor change a single thing. Other than calling that being a man, you might also say that it is all much like walking around in darkness as shown here in this work done largely with ink on paper.

**Grandfather Winston**

After South Dakota it seemed like the time to do family research, so I gathered as much of the past as was available. For a while, it seemed that it was the only thing that mattered. Then I got out my pencils, sketch board, a smooth board wide enough to hold the paper, and pencils, charcoal pencils, stick charcoal, kneaded eraser, and several kneaded erasers that pick-up lots of carbon. This work was done in 1993 and 1994.

This drawing became a second Walker´s Girl to me, but more like The Country Doctor with a smile. I remember him so well, so vividly even though I moved away when I was six years of age and missed the last ten years of his life. Winston Rouw deserves a note of honor: He was called Dutch by everyone and he farmed on his own, farmed on shares, and later managed farms for others for most of his life. That means he was a farmer, first, last and everything in between.

Grandpa Winston lost his left arm to a machine that left only a stub until the day he died, just south of Fort Smith, Arkansas. He loved to smile, he loved to tell stories and tales, he loved to sit on the front porch and talk with friends and family and relax in the shade. I would wager that most people who knew him also respected him if not loved him. He was that kind of man.

What is a man, anyway? What is a good man? To me it depends on your definition of goodness.  But how you do you define a man. There are some exceptions to the rule, but I find that most men are in an altered state of mind when they come up face to face with a remarkably beautiful woman. The woman doesn´t have to be all that beautiful. They can just have ¨that look¨ and most men become instantly lost at sea. I know there are many exceptions, but that is now it looks to me in a nutshell: you get lost in attraction.

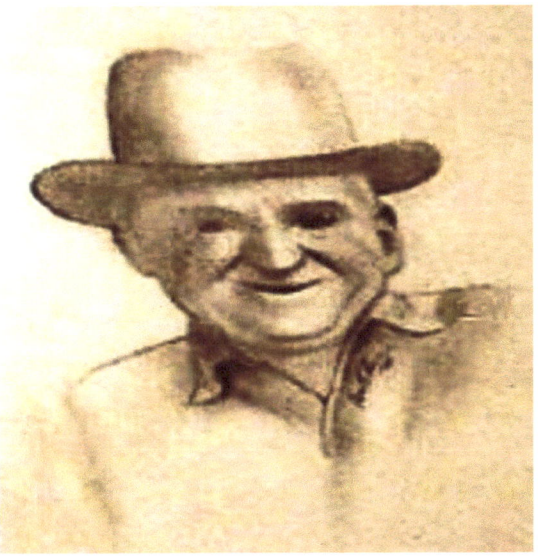

**Nellie Wave**

Nellie Wave Waltermeyer Rouw lived about ten years longer than her husband. She spent her later years traveling back and forth to California to see her children. Unfortunately, when her stamina wore away, she wound up in a nursing home. I remember visiting her and witnessing the strength and determination in her face. She was a force in so many of the lives in the family.

Several family members had moved to California and they needed visiting with just like the ones that stayed home in Arkansas. I think it is safe to say that she ruled every roost she was in. She acted and lived as if she was stronger than dirt. If you want to see what "right" looks like, just look in her eyes.

The technical issues with this drawing are its use of light and darkness in contrast. I also changed my drawing style to spend more time just putting myself in the shoes of the person being drawn. Then the question becomes one of finding the right contrast. Contrast grabs the attention of the eyes and reveals character like nothing else will. It is a key in all portrait drawings, drawings, as well as paintings and photographs.

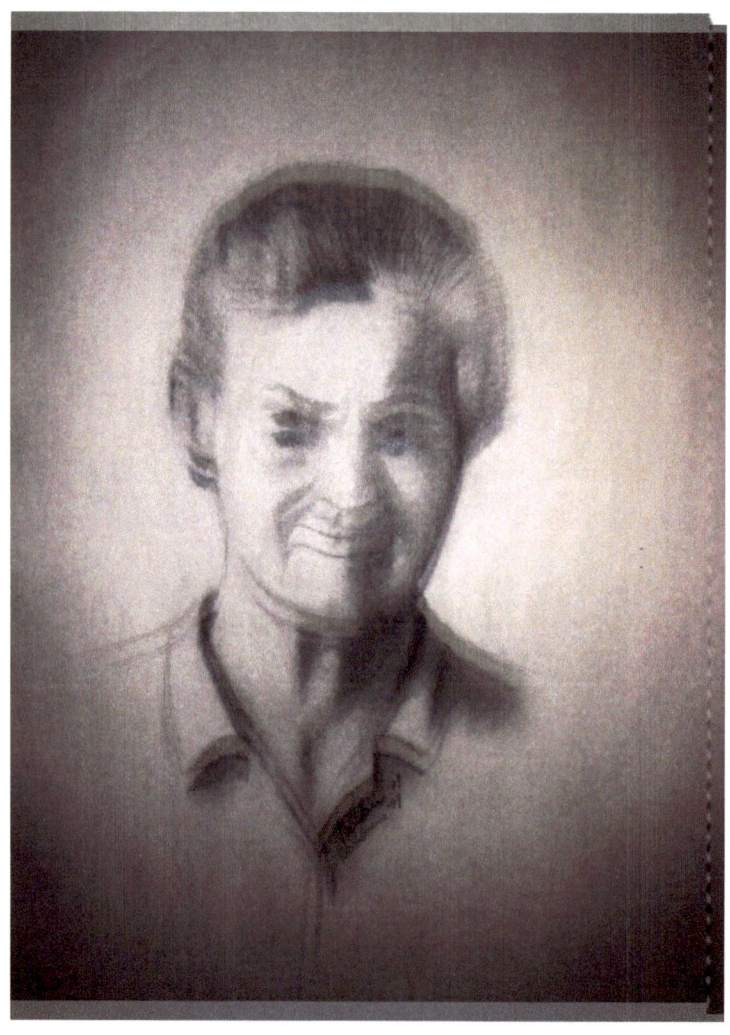

## Big Grins

### 1995

This is an impression of how Marilyn Monroe looked to me. Yes, she was like a slice of angel-food cake that smiled as if there was no tomorrow. Yes, she grew up in times during the Great Depression, as it was commonly known as and she grew up within eyesight of the giant HOLLYWOOD billboard that sits on the hill overlooking Los Angeles. She saw it from her well-fenced suburban home and no doubt dreamed of stardom and all the illusions that go with it. She didn't keep a diary that I knew of or even want to keep a diary. She had only her dreams, but they left quite a record. Who would not want to live out their childhood dreams? It was later said that she became tangled up in fame. That is certainly one way to account for sad ending. Sad to see.

This old photo of the work suffered some damages over the year, unfortunately, but if there was ever a cheesecake made in heaven, its name was surely Norma Jean Baker, aka Marilyn Monroe.

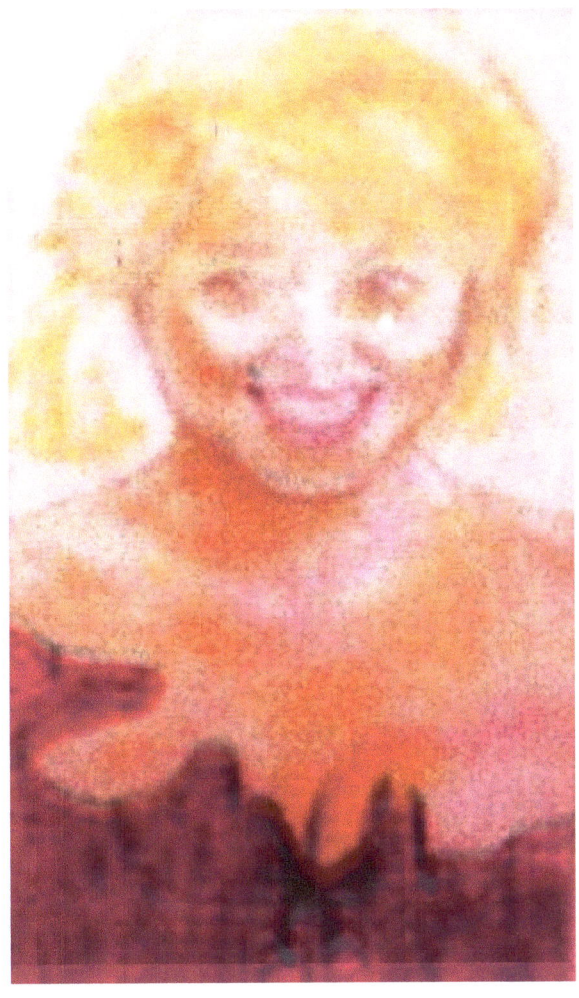

**Still Life with Limes 1995**

This was done during a period of love for Vincent Van Gogh and his method of painting. This is an oil on canvas painting of a pot perched weirdly on a tabletop with limes. It is a simple still life, but it came to hold lots of meaning for me. It is simple in composition and shows my adopted and adapted flowing brush strokes. At the time they reminded me of the flow found in Van Gogh. You could say that I copied his style, but that is a self-congratulatory way to think of it. Still, I do like to remember it that way. It does have some umber and burnt umber colors mixed with the earthen tones of the big round jug. I captured the jug in full, I thought. I find the pot to be engaging… as if you wanted to embrace it. It may not have that much of appeal or be that engaging to you. But to me, it is an appealing painting.

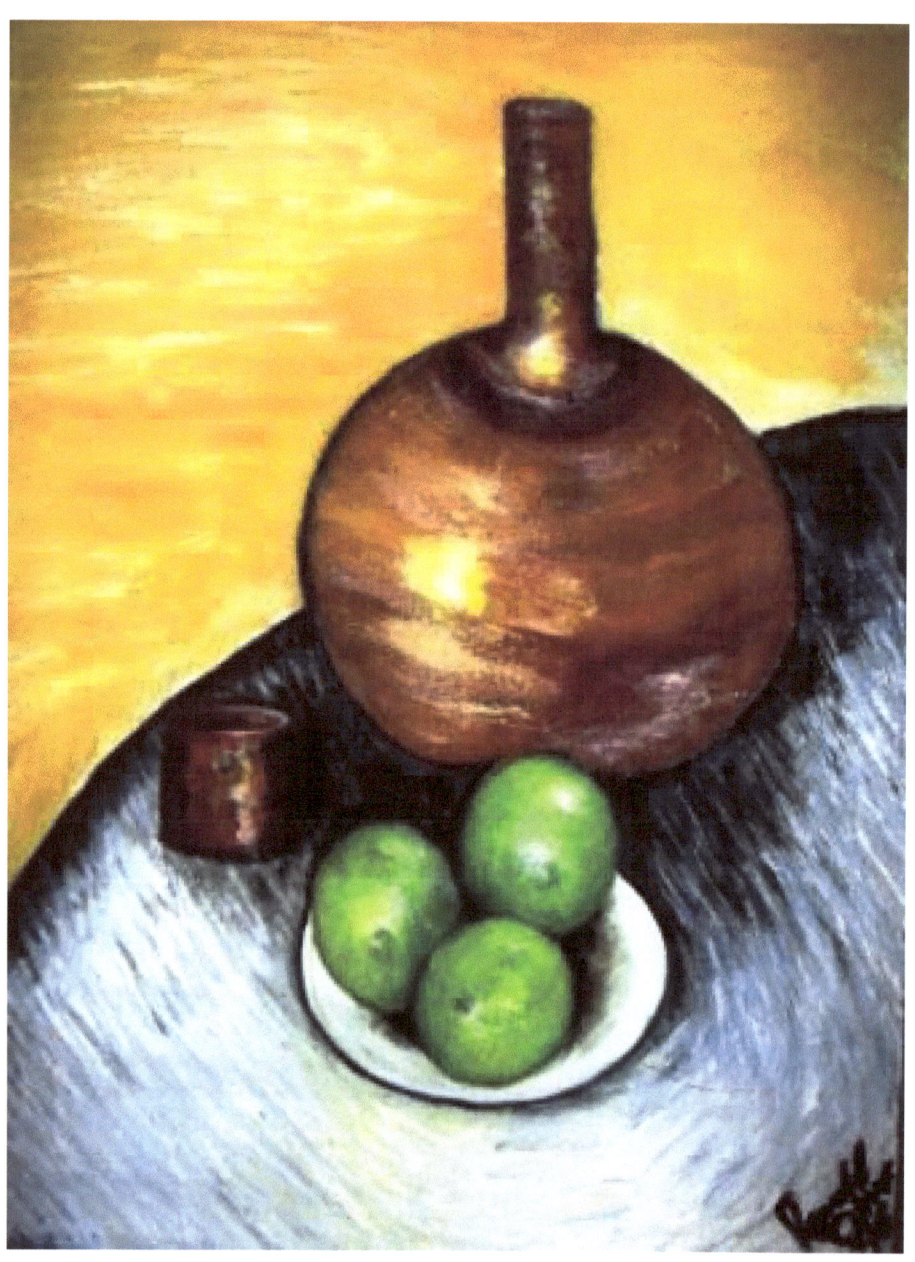

**Madonna and Child 1996**

This was done during a time of increasing abstraction of forms that went beyond reality. By this I mean that there was no one-to-one correspondence between the image on canvas and anything seen in the outer-stylized world. It was a time of trying to think in terms of essence and then putting that spiritual essence on canvas in a form that would look appealing, at least in some way.

I am thinking that portrait artists have long known that one day their work would go out of style. I am guessing that they knew a camera was possible long before it was a reality. The ¨artists¨ knew that one day an invention that might put them out of business. I have read story after story about the inevitable death of all finer art in the face of the new technology. I don´t believe most of it. Art is much more deeply connected to human life and culture for that to happen. Still, the question was being asked if cameras did not give a much more accurate and faithful copy of life? They clearly do have a reliable texture, a standard size and likeness that impresses nearly everyone. How could any portrait artist hope to compete with such perfection? Perhaps the greatest appeal of the camera was that this machine could do a small miracle in a moment´s time instead of over a period of weeks and months of time. Who does not like to save time?

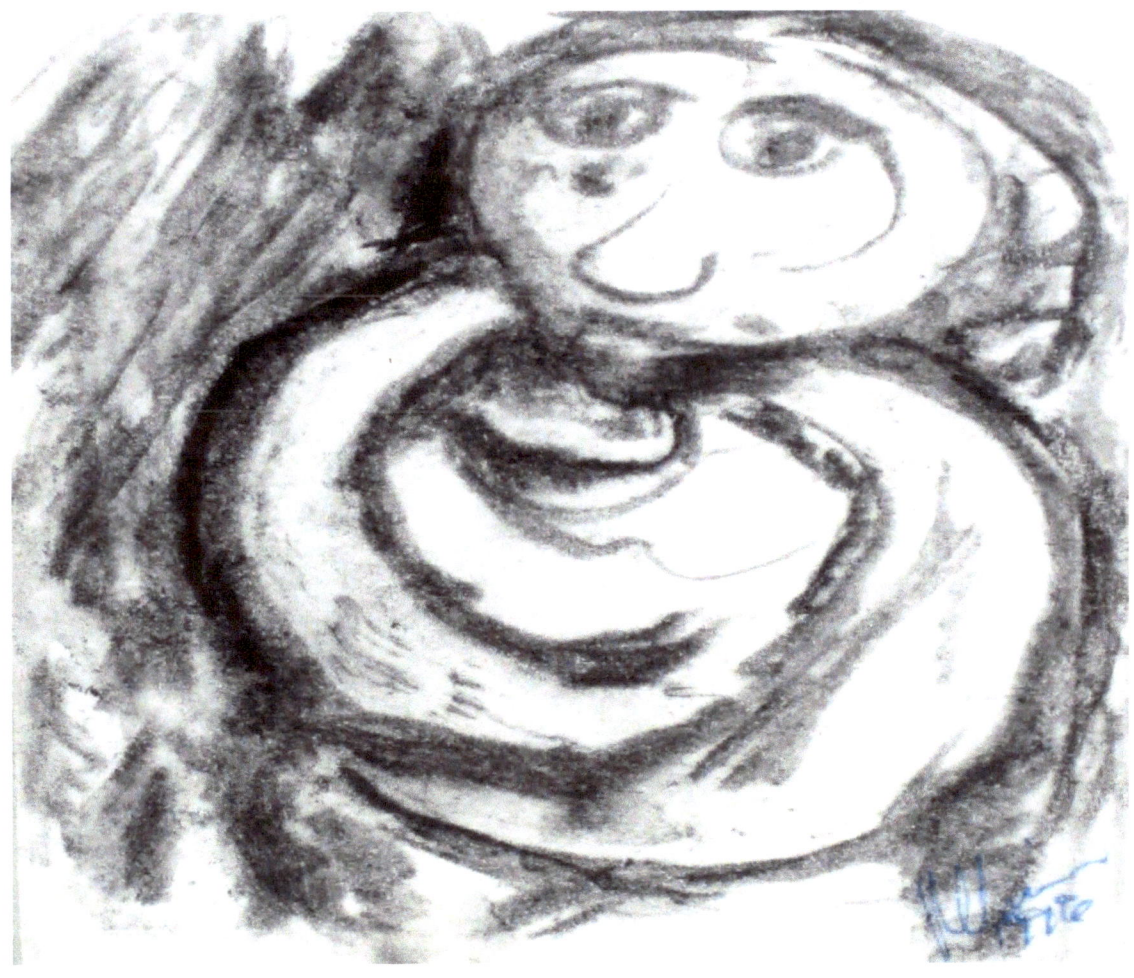

## Smell This - 1994

When I moved back to Tulsa finally in 1994 it felt good to be home, or what seemed like my home since early childhood. I had lived two years near the West Coast in Washington State and was ready for slow speech and down-home humour that you only find in Oklahoma, or so it seemed at the time. I was wanting to find a permanent home, but I did not find it. When all is said and done, I was not a success in Richland, Washington, though I gave it my best shot. What more is there to say other than my professional career started to take a backseat to my artistic interests.

The work was done in chalk pastels and charcoal on paper. It showed two delighted boys playing in the spring greenery in the park across the street from the apartment where I lived. The boys ran and ran and rested only to inhale the smell of flowers. There was no doubt that they loved their play together. You could almost smell it. It seemed like the flowers had their own bouquet. The flowers had an aroma you could almost take in and they were complemented by the whiff of grass being mowed grass. The boys seemed lost in amazement. The name for it was obvious: Here, Smell This. I first called it by its abbreviated title and still do.

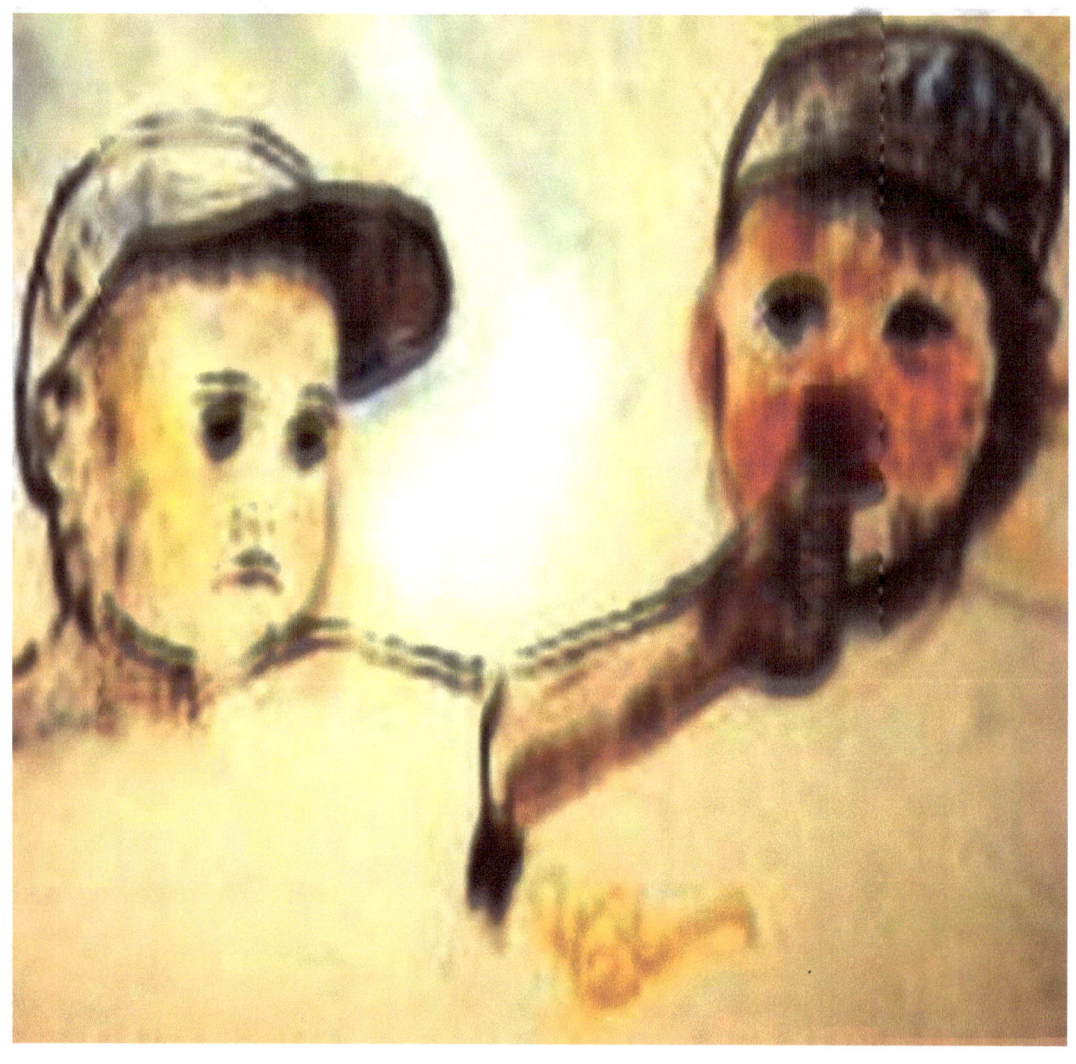

# The Child in the Basement 1995

I was in a different state of mind when I drew this mixed media work. I started out looking at a very well-contrasted photograph. The photographer remarked that it was the best work he had ever done with a camera. I thought so, too. I wanted the drawing to be in the same league. I remember him as being so proud of the work. Then I stared at it for the longest time and got to a different level of the image. It was like walking into the image, getting on the floor with it and then walking back out but leaving a friend to keep my new friend company. I went totally into the image with both hands and eyes that did the drawing. It was not "touched up" until I had a final product. I can say that it is not the boy I started with. This boy was in pain and instead of a celebration of fatherhood, I was looking at the abandonment of hope. The story by Ursula Le Guinn, "The Boy in the Basement" immediately came to mind.

How did I know to turn the feet inwards? I do not remember. I was later told it was true to the reality of a severely neglected child.

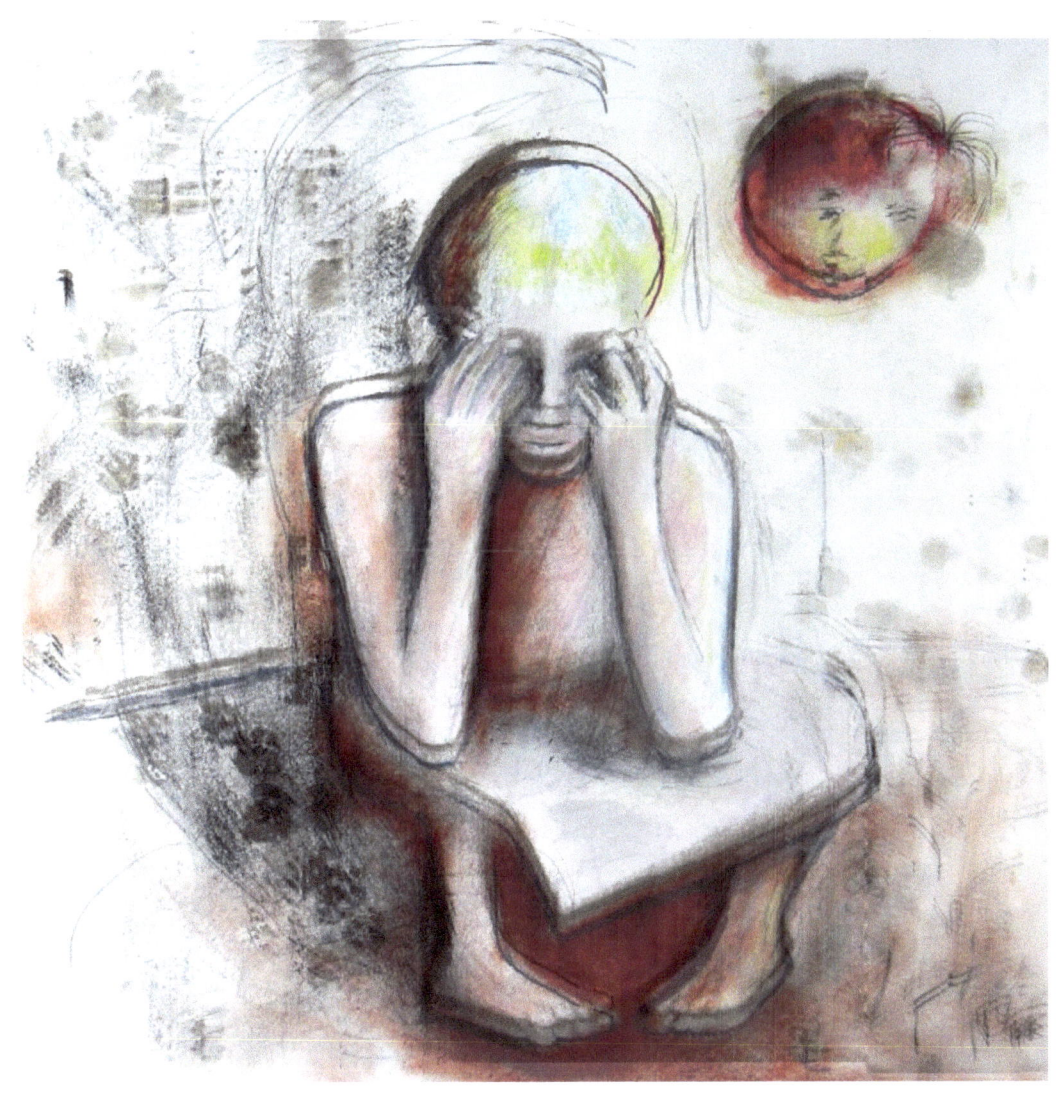

**The Searcher – 1996**

I did this drawing on a dried coffee filter in about the middle of a six-month period from April of 1996 to October 1996. I was living in the Barcelona Apartments in Tulsa and a large public park, LaFortune Park was across the street. I was living roughly ten miles from the streets of the northside where I grew up. I left my career as a grant writer and behavioural consultant in my rear-view mirror to study drawing and painting as never before. I painted and drew on everything at hand all day long. The routine lasted for six months from daylight to dusk. I loved the freedom and opportunity to do what felt so right. And the change of pace was like breathing totally clean air.

I remember drinking a lot of coffee at all hours of the day and night. I was raised not to waste anything. This state of heightened awareness applied to the coffee filters and they took on their own fascination. Over time I realized that when coffee filters dried, they took on a second life as they made good paper for drawing on with pastel chalk, charcoal, or even acrylic paint. This is one of about twenty coffee filter works I did from that time and I called it ¨The Searcher.¨

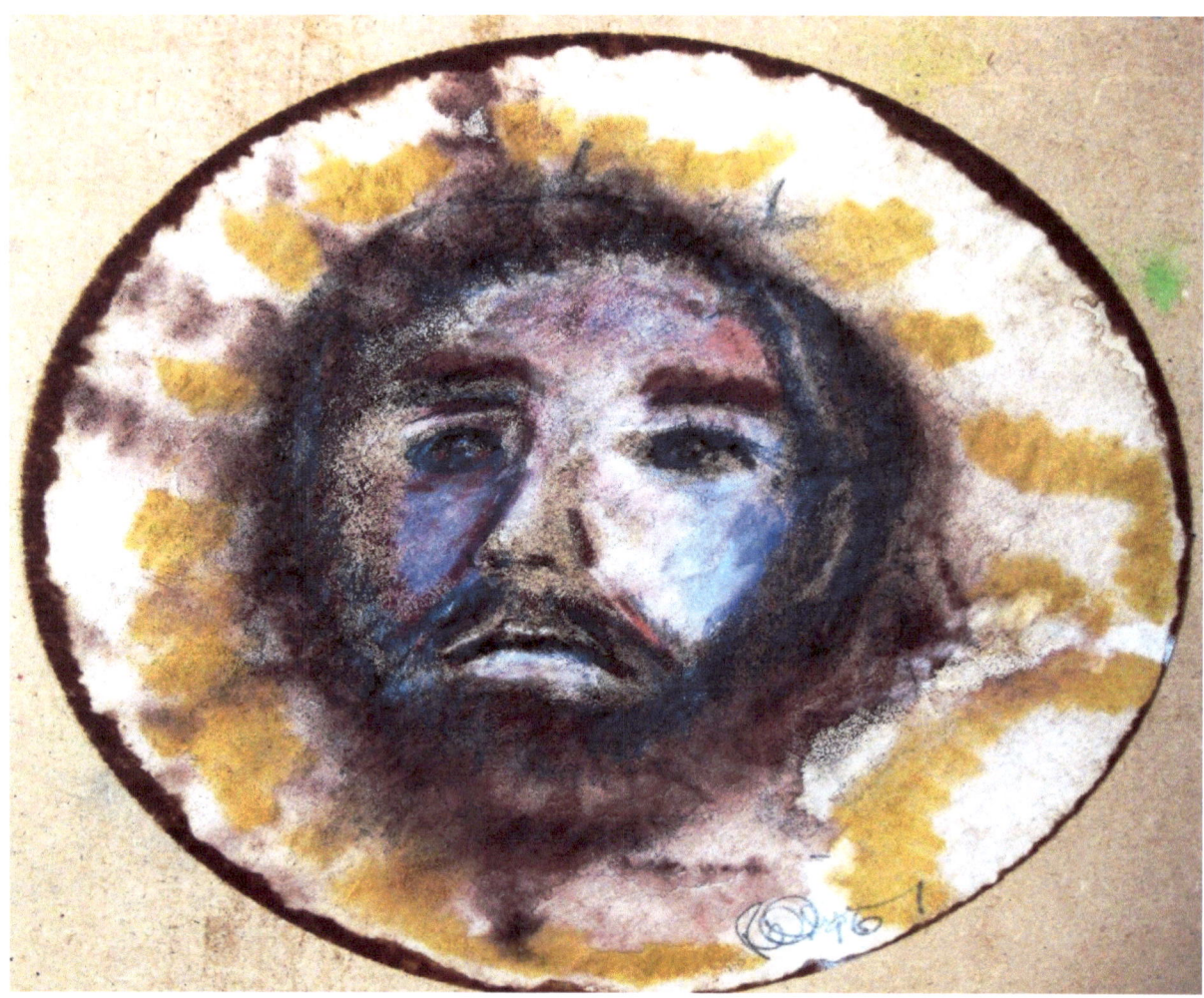

**Colorado 1997**

This was done on canvas after the style of Bob Ross, meaning trees painted mostly with slash marks with his trademark big brush. In case you have had the misfortune to have never seen Bob Ross paint you should know that he was most friendly. He shared all he knew. He shared everything on the how-to side of things and talks lovingly to his work as if he had a relationship with it. Even with use of oversized brushes, he did lots of delicate painting with touches of free-handed dabbling. His trees were always composed of a series of downward slashes, but he was aware of the need for visual variety. I came to think that he tried to see the finished product all the time he worked on it. His paintings did always look well-composed and with attention given to the smallest detail. He did use tiny brushes for some bark and branch details but usually even the smallest details were done with his one-inch brushes that grew to two or three inches at times.

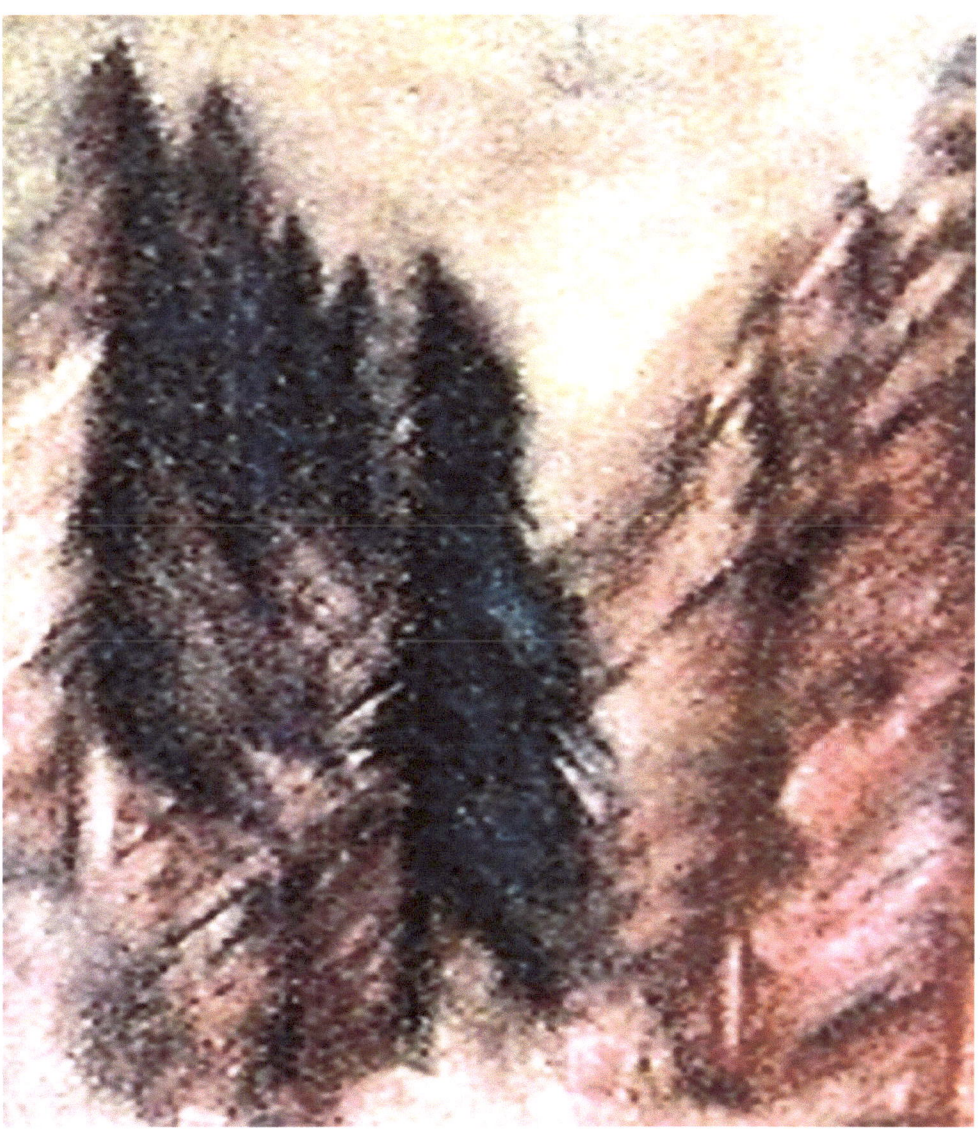

## A Cabin in the Pines 1989

I did this while living outside of Vermilion, South Dakota near the banks of the Missouri River. It shows an imaginary home in the Black Hills, a cabin in the pines done with pastel on paper. I used toilet paper and my fingers to do most of the blending and the wispiness of the smoke was considered a victory over an adversary at the time. I remember celebrating the finishing accomplishment. All my life I had wanted to live in such a home and at last I could. I still think it is ideal.

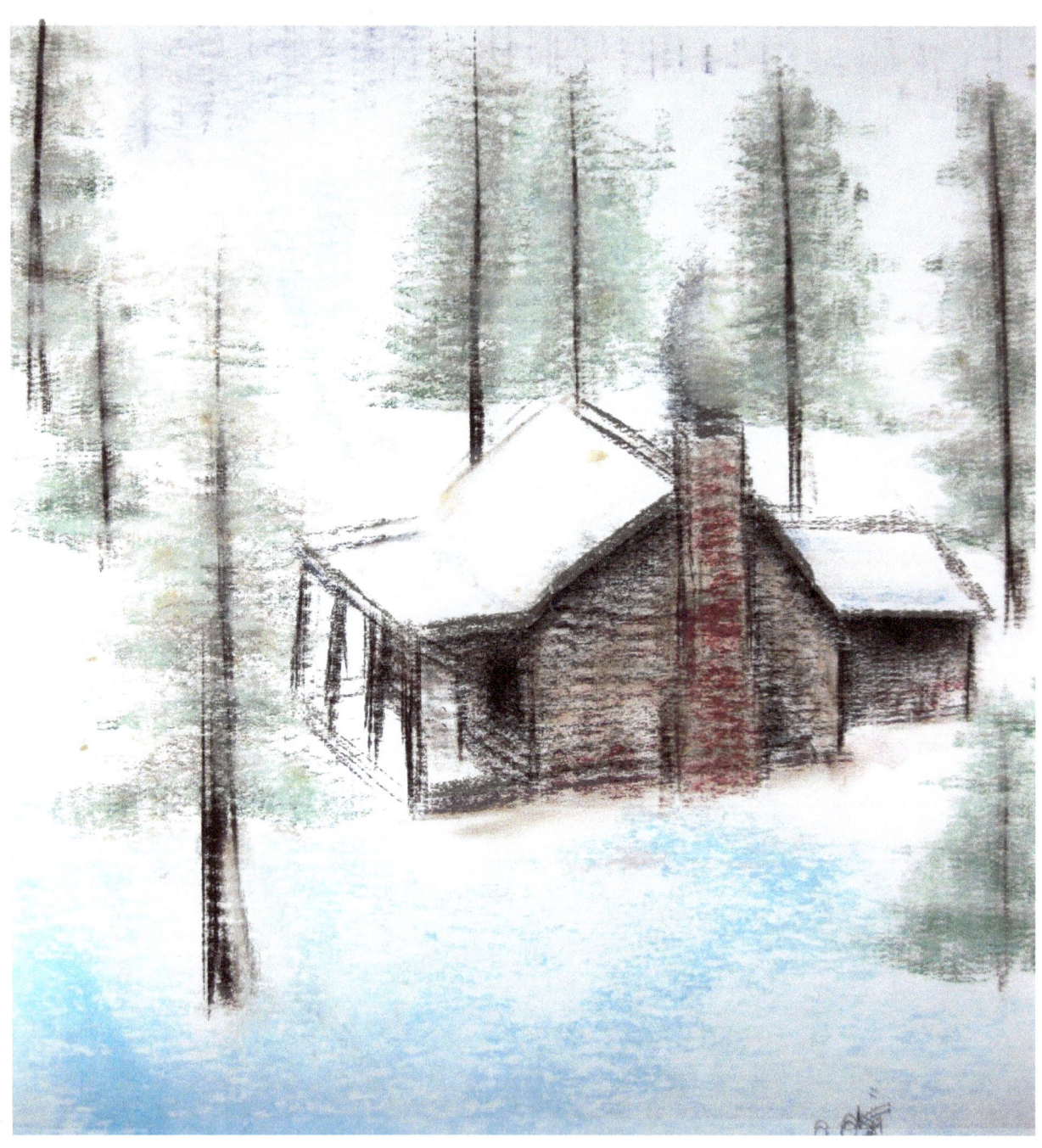

**Abstract 161 – 1996**

I clearly remember sitting on the floor with my pad of paper in front of me and my box of pastels to one side and just tackling this work. I was looking at the universe inside of me and remembering the words of Karl Jung that "The best way to understand the universe within is to understand the universe without." So, I thought it was time to express that expansive feeling on paper. It has a wide variety of colors that are used in an order that seemed different, so I called it an **Abstract Universe**, or just **Abstract 161**:

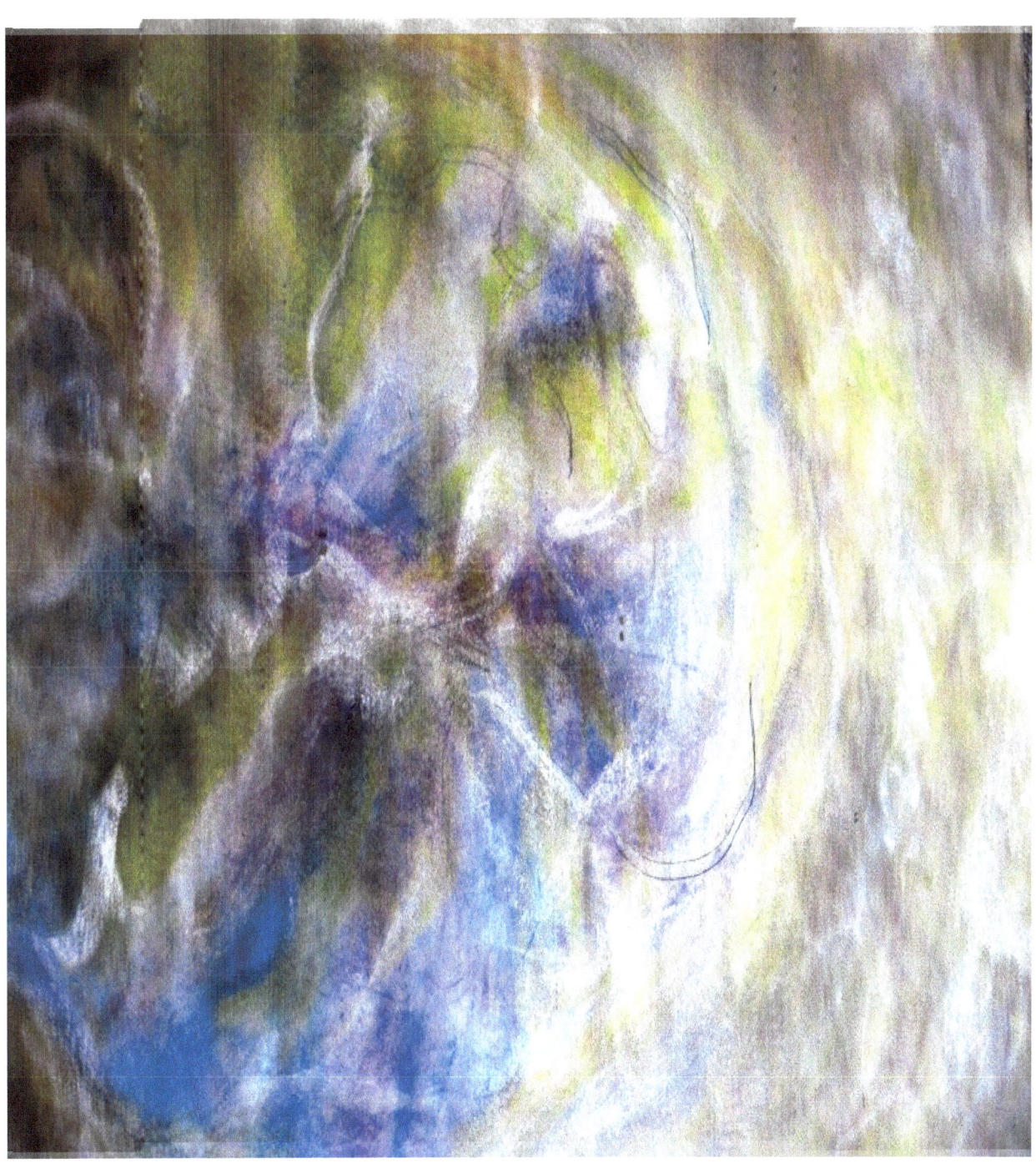

**Drawing Mother 1997**

While waiting for a job to develop I moved in the home of my mother for several months. Of course, I asked myself how an adult in their late forties could even consider moving back home. I thought of myself as failing in the life I pursued and needed to start over. Moving back home for even several months put me in the loser category when the need to find out about the unexplored parts of life were closer to the truth.

To take my mind off the dilemma I picked up my pencil and drew my mother sitting in her chair watching the television and perhaps pondering her take on things. She had a definite talent for pondering. I think I caught the mood, the personality trait with this drawing. I sat in a one-down position to approximate the tone of the drawing. I was looking up to her face when I drew her. She always wanted to be above the battle, though that was not possible all the time. Regardless, she showed me the expression she brought with her.

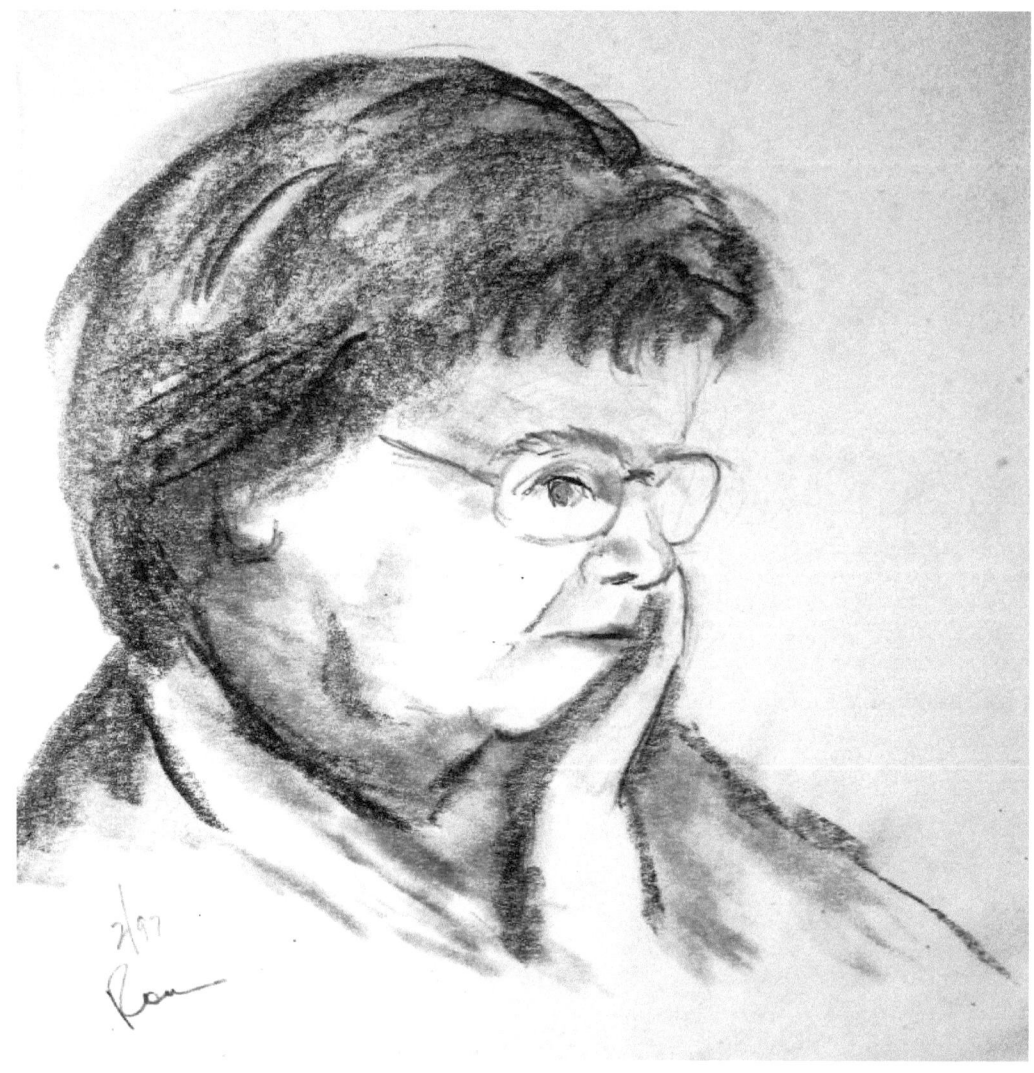

**Yellow Maraca** 2013

This was done with watercolor on paper and was one of the first paintings I did after moving to Colombia in 2004. I had not had a class as such in watercolor in my earlier training, so I decided it was time to study watercolors. Ms. Lilia Yepes, a Professor of Fine Art at the Univesidad del Valle here, showed me the way to watercolors and left me marvelling at her wells of her talent. Her studio was named was called Two Spaces or Espacio Dos and it was only a couple of blocks from where I lived. I studied watercolor painting with her for two years. When I started thinking of painting as a second career, she told me with complete confidence that it was ¨almost impossible¨ to make a living from personal artwork as the market was so poor. That took the pressure to sell and succeed off. Her thinking was that completed works were best sold in Miami, Florida where there was a renowned art market built for that purpose.

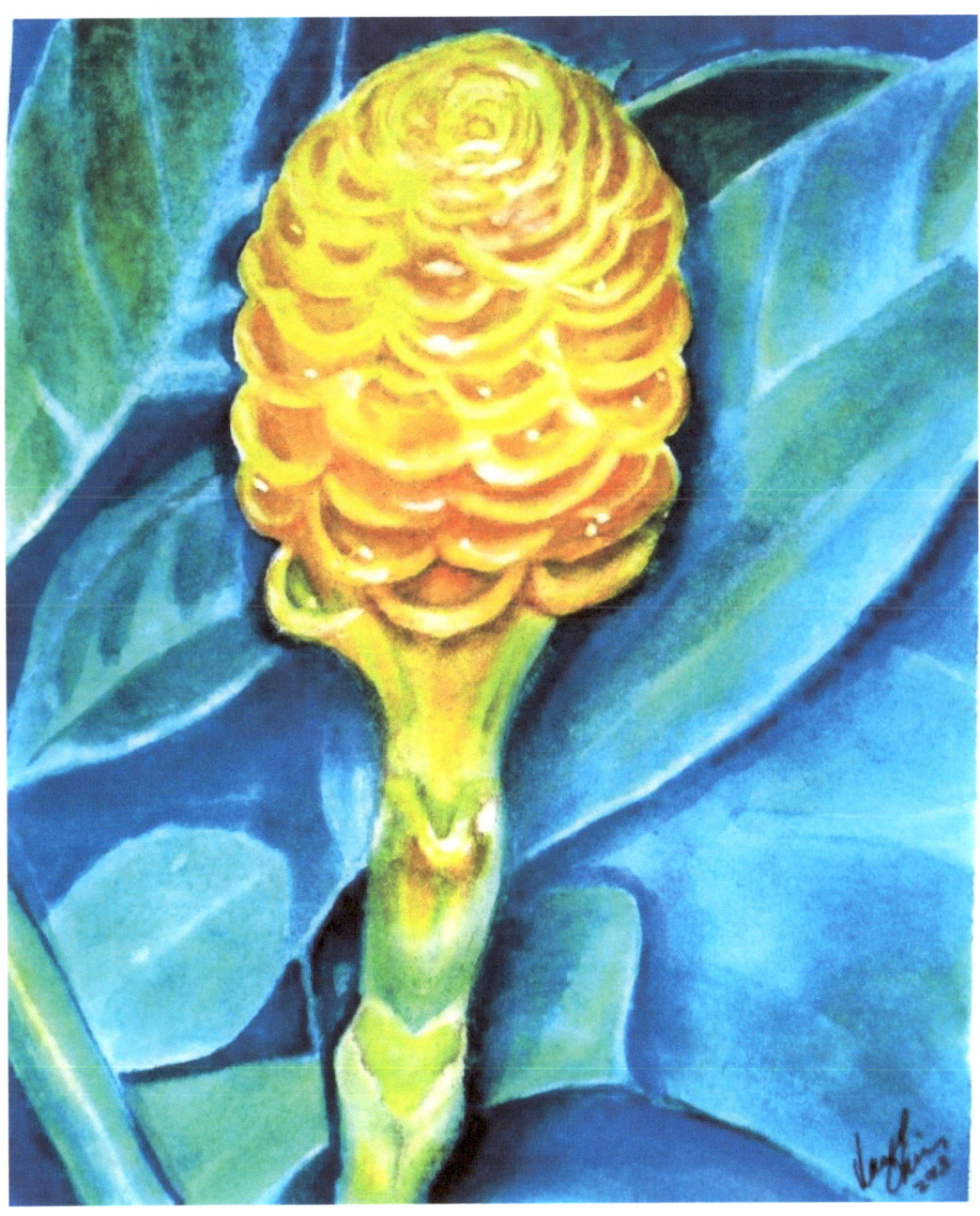

## Flor Bromelia – 2013

Bromeliads are known here as bromelias. Regardless, they are known to be an epiphyte, a plant that lives off others. That is, plants that grow on other plants. I was struck by them first in Popayan, a colonial capital known as the White City. We stayed at a nice hotel where they had bromelias growing profusely growing in their yards and tree groves. I knew at once that I had to paint them and there are some old photographs posted on my Facebook site that shows what I worked from. This work was done in the middle of the second year of study. It had taken me time to develop skills in watercolor but they came slowly but surely. I found it to be an interesting media as it is about transparency and intensity of color. I experimented and discovered that by using drops of glycerin I could brighten the color. It still hangs on the wall of my home and I still take great pride in having done it.

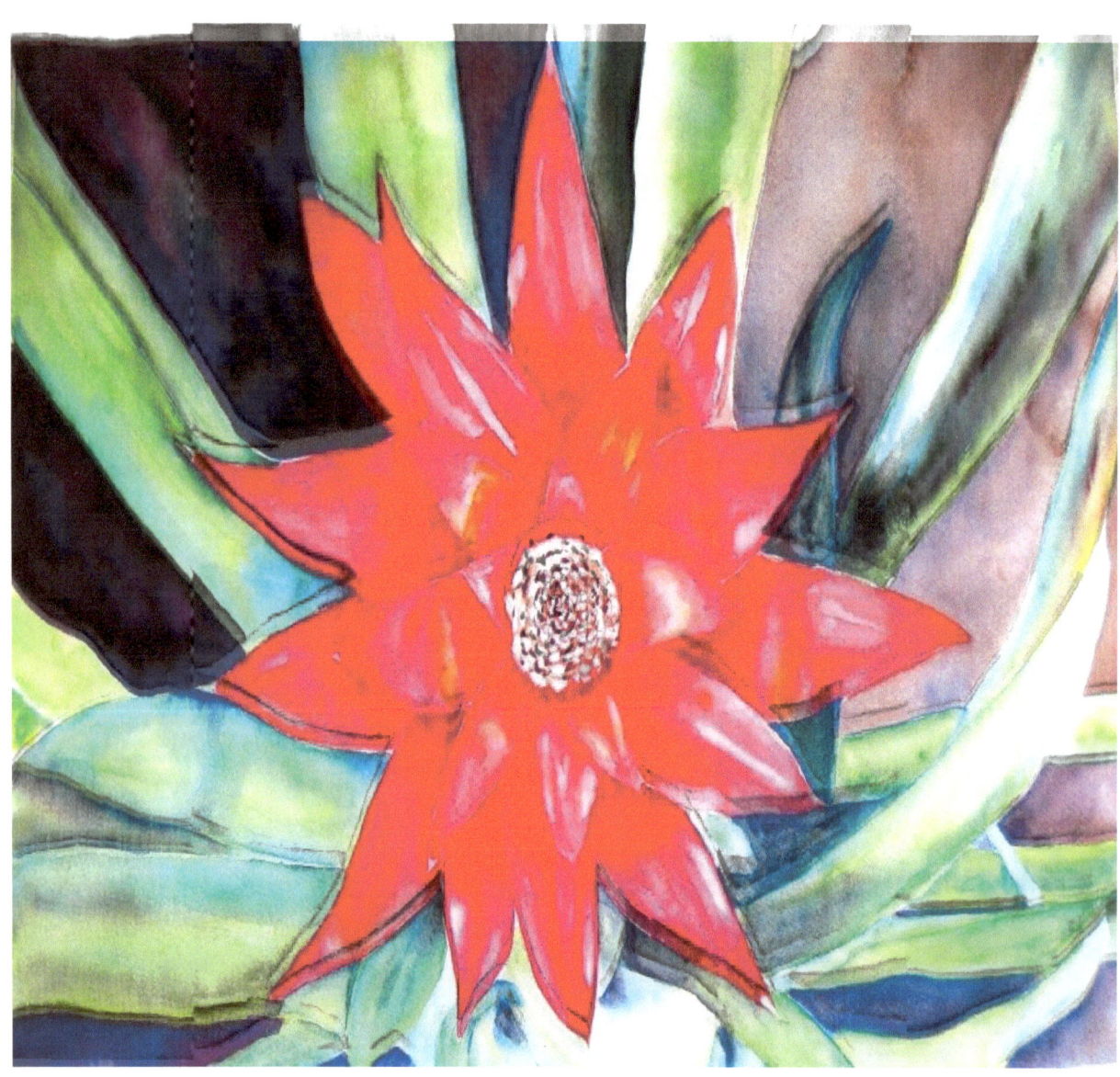

## Let's Go Fly a Bike 2014

This work makes me smile every time I see it. It is a happy work and started from seeing a bicycle perched on a building near the city center by the Roman arches of Queretero, Mexico. There was a street sweeper that also caught my attention as looking as hard as nails while meticulously doing her work. I tried repeatedly but could not capture that look.

I remember buying a new straight edge and T-square before I began this drawing because I wanted to emphasize the straight lines of the colonial-styled building it was perched on. I had never been there before, so I was taking it all in and looking forward to the longer stay in San Miguel de Allende. This work still makes me smile. I had the Mary Poppins song in my mind while drawing. "Let's Go Fly a Kite", so why not fly a bike? Where I got the oranges for wheels, I could not say, other than whimsy.

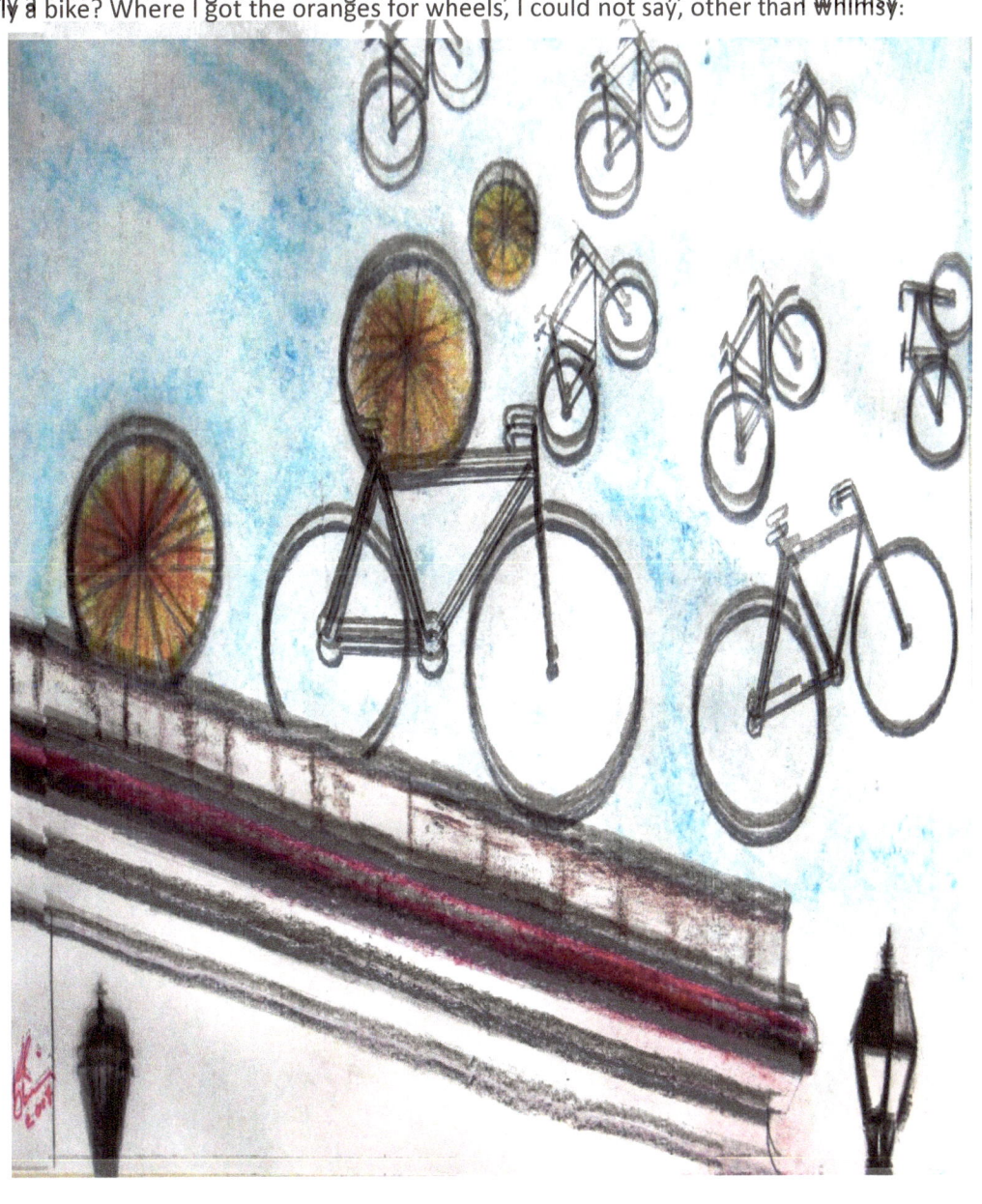

**A Colombian Girl from Yumbo 2014**

For several years people I respect in art have told me that this is the best painting I had ever done before they saw it. At the time I did it I was thinking of watercolors and how much easier and quicker and more controlled if the watercolor was first applied in the form of a pencil. I started this one with those pencils. From there I applied regular watercolors and made it twice as vibrant. If you don´t believe me just ask the little girl that posed for this photograph. She remembers it well and loved it from the start. So much so that I eventually just gave it to her. I felt like a lonely-hearts club member overcoming the stacked odds and winning.

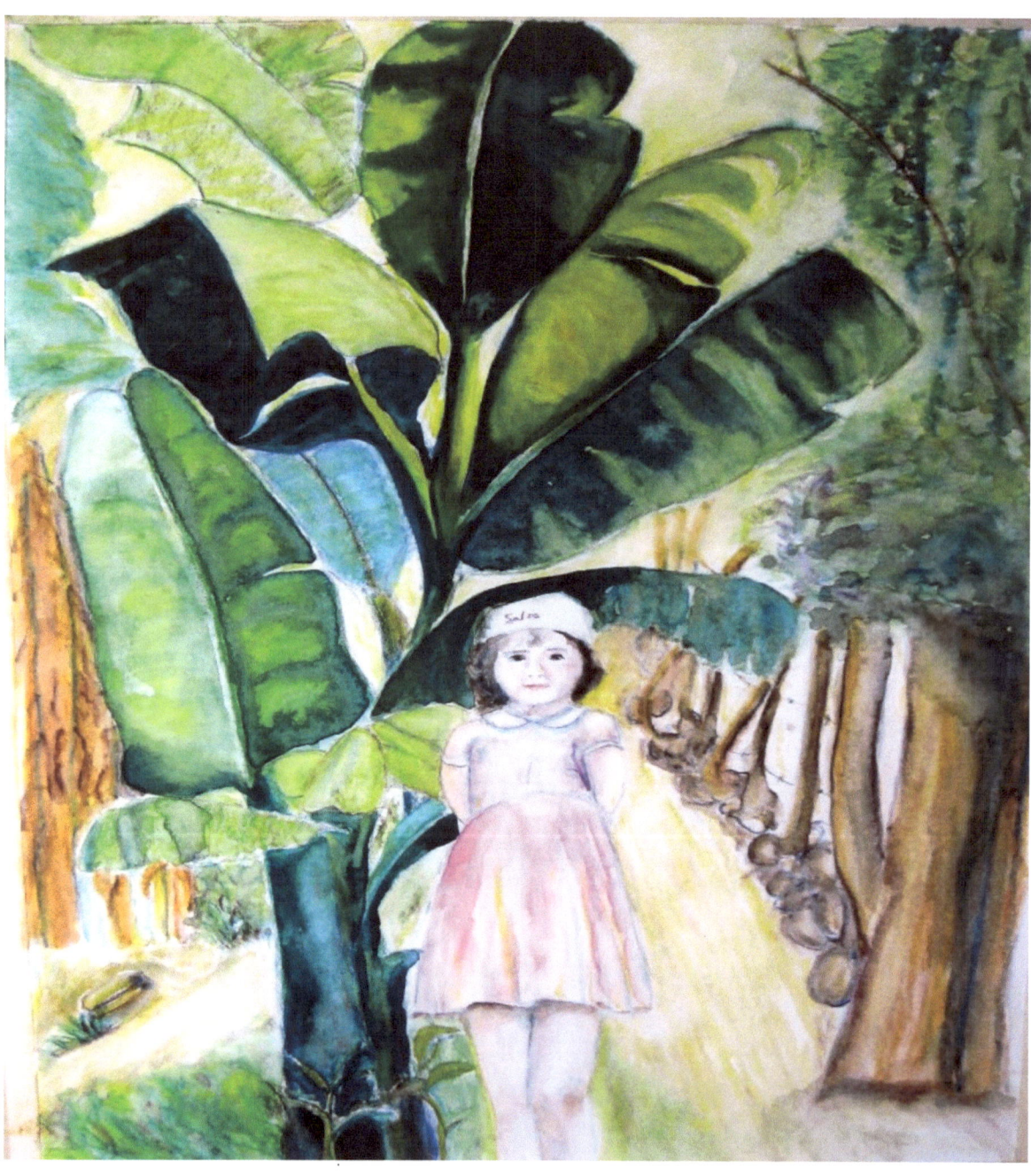

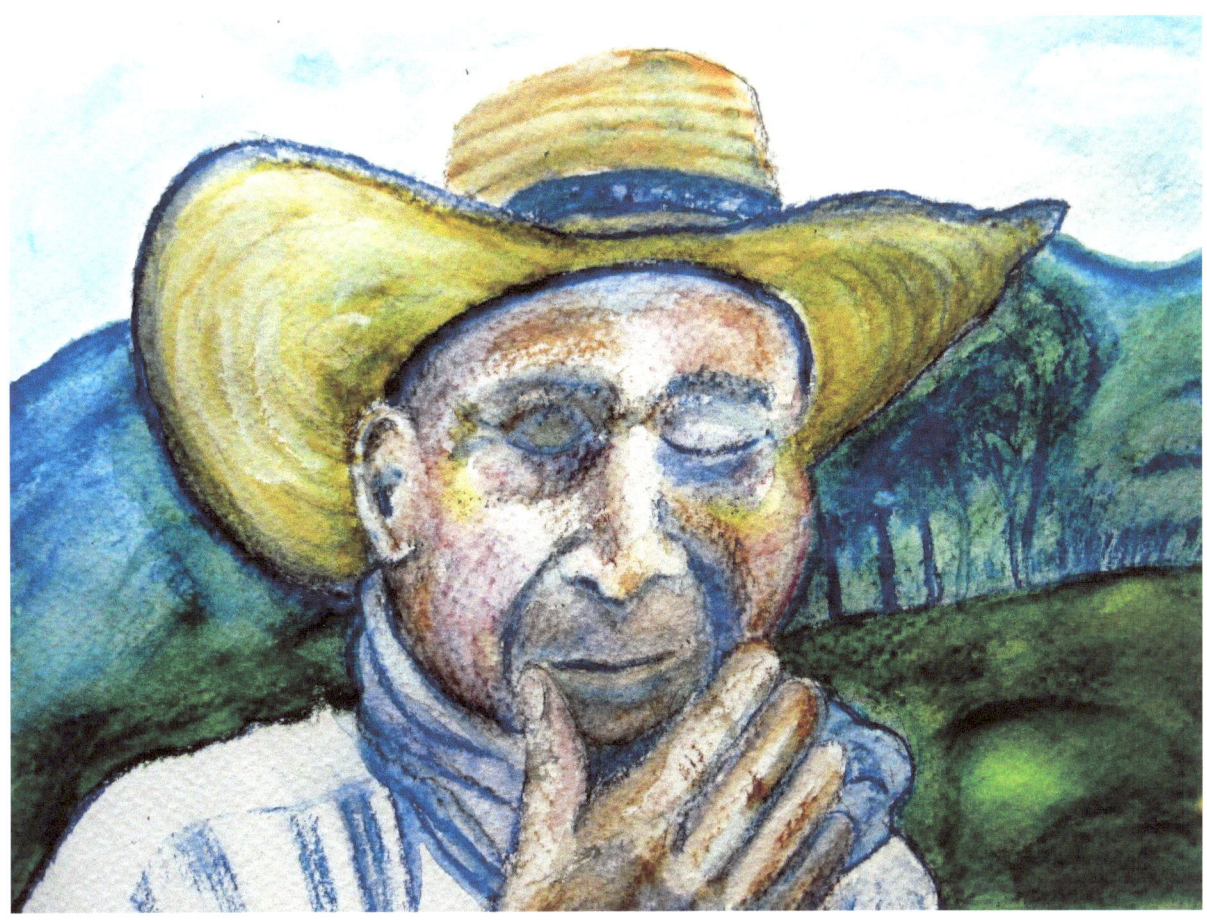

**The Crying Campesino**

This was done in watercolor and featured a photograph from the local newspaper. I thought the photographer caught the emotion of the moment that was hard to overlook. To me it captured the essence of defeat and loss. Strong emotion captures attention. This image always seemed strong to me and highly expressive. The unexpected element also holds your eyes, e.g. a man in pain shedding tears. It pulls you out of yourself, which is also called human empathy and compassion. You join the figure and pray for a better tomorrow.

## Displaced 2015

I asked a neighbourhood fixture to pose for a drawing and he was eager from the start. First, he told me his story and I figured him for an escape artist. In his younger days he had both of his parents killed by the guerrilla and he ran from the hills of Cauca to his new home in Cali. Cali was not only a much bigger city but offered hope and promise of a better life. His work is as a vigilante in front of a bakery school that provides oversight to parked cars and empty parking spaces. You could find him every morning filling the air with praises of the smell of fresh bread from the oven and heaping praise on the cooking students. He could not get enough satisfaction from of being the best vigilante on the street.

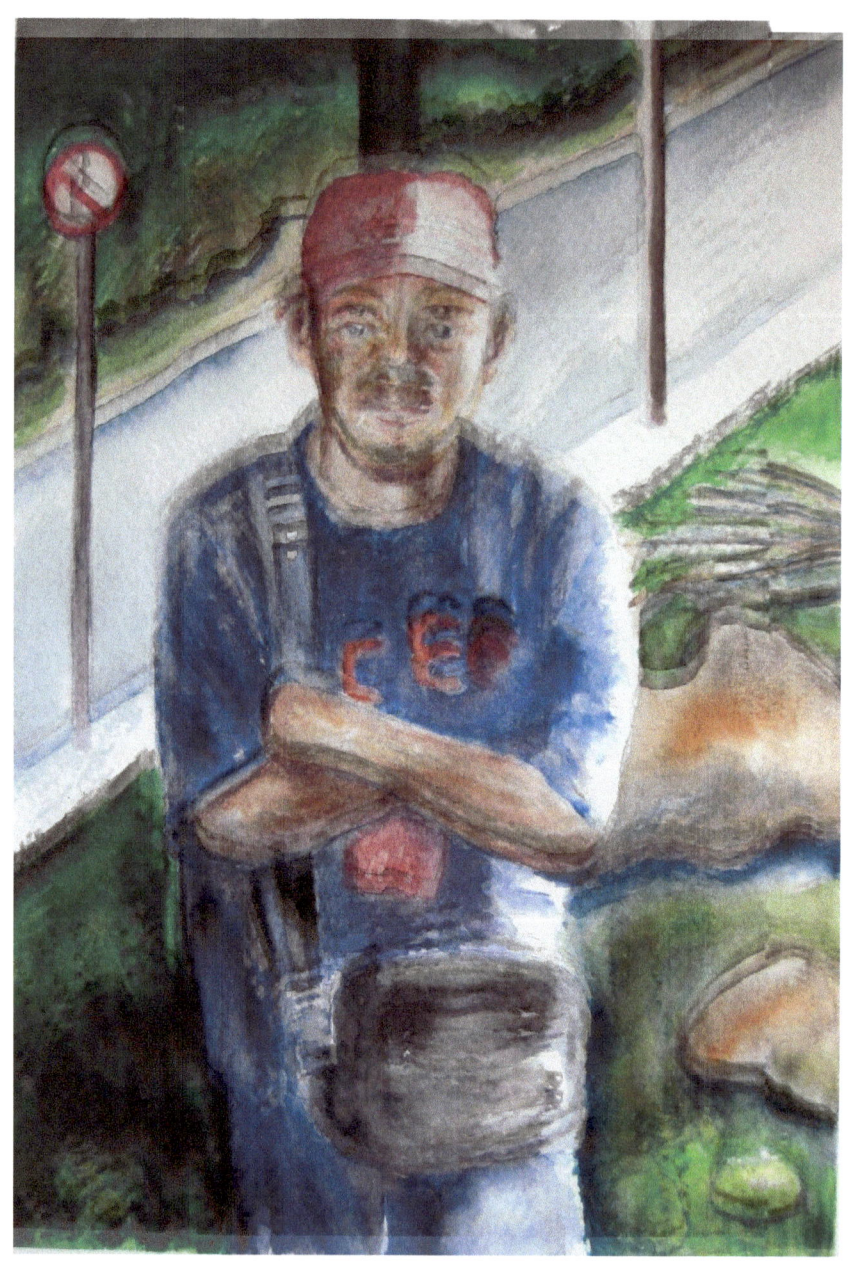

# El Silletero Feliz (The Happy Flower Carrier)

This one has an interesting story behind it. As Medellin is widely known as a garden city, home of yellow flowers and festivals for *guayacanes*, it is also known as the top gathering place for flower venders, also known as *silleteros*. They come down from the high mountains in the spring to bring blooming greenery and flowers to every less fortunate city dweller who has money enough to buy the best and the freshest.

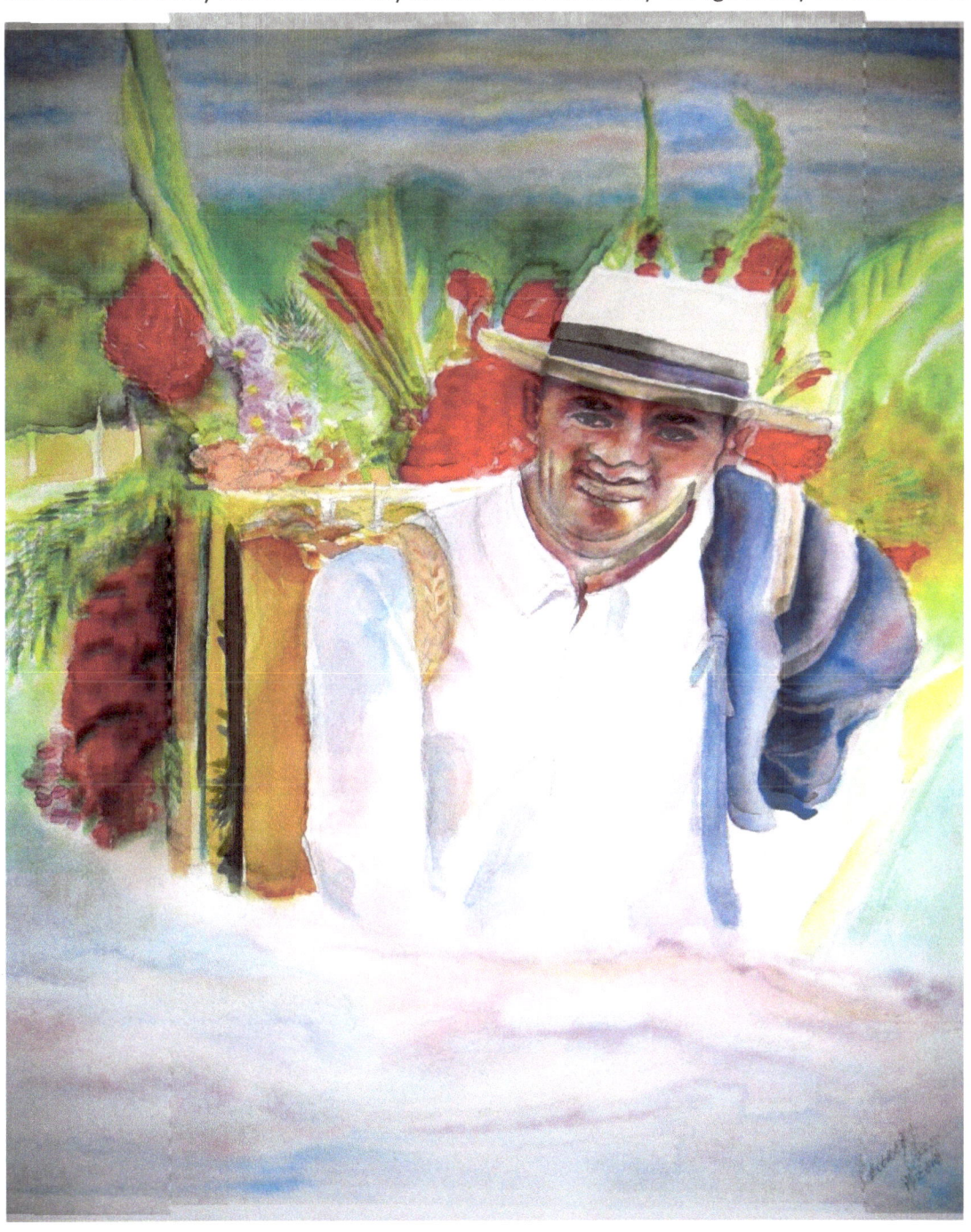

**The Washerwoman**

This is a drawing of the Washerwoman, the mother of the only President of Colombia that I have uncovered who is known for having humble origins, Marcus Fidel Suarez. Her wrinkled and arthritic hands immediately caught my attention. I studied the history of Colombia and went on to read that Marcus Suarez was educated by the Catholic Church and started the Colombian Air Force. He led the way in thinking about planes and mail and passenger service. With the help of German funding

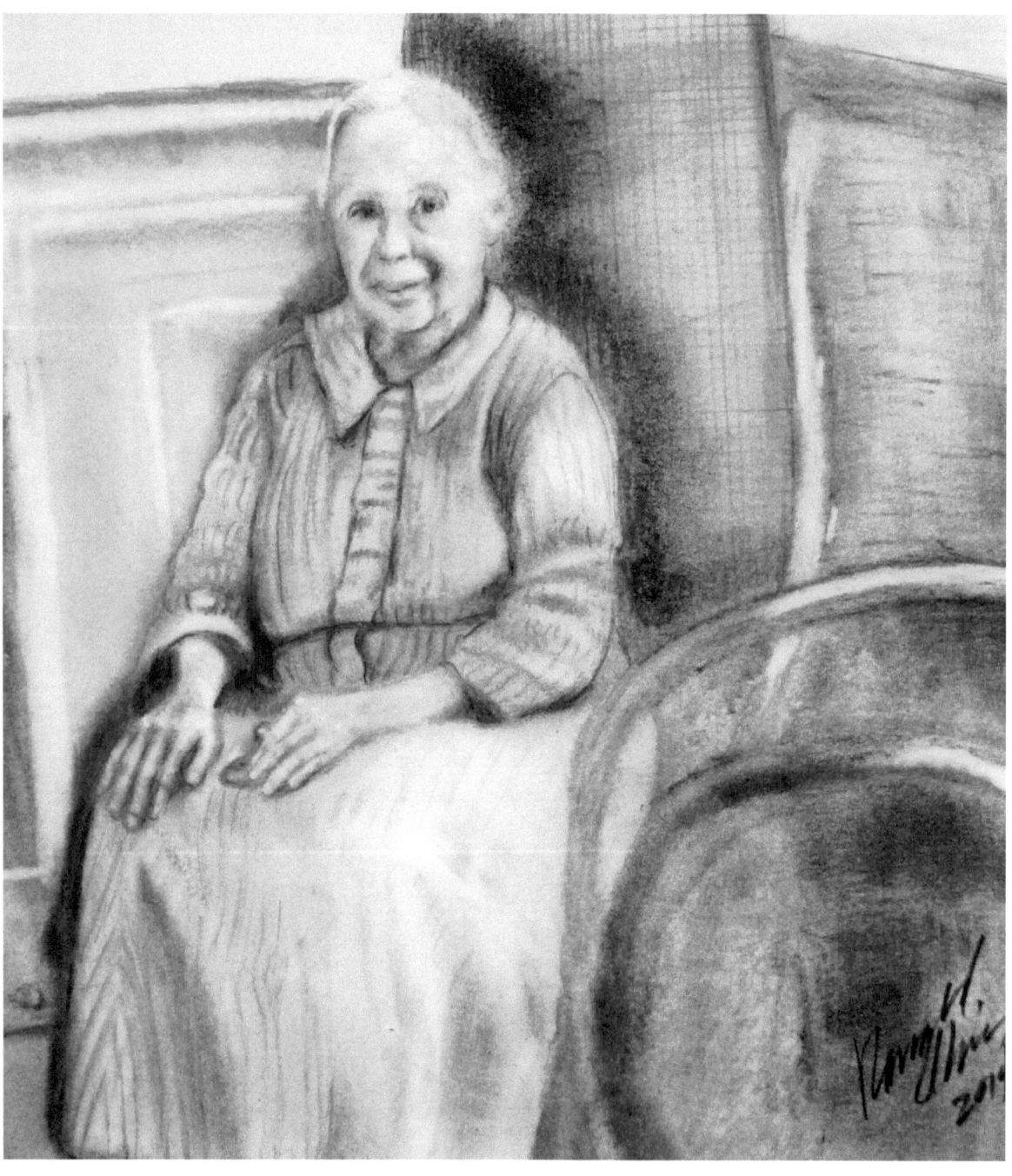

Colombia was second only to Britain in leading in the use of the airplane. Being socially isolated by three ranges of the Andes mountains was a driving force. The Air Force Base in Cali is named after this distinguished man of humble origin.

This woman knew that education would be the key for her son´s future. She permitted her boy to stand in the window outside the school room and listen to the words of the teacher. He clearly loved to learn and took advantage of every opportunity to do so. I have no doubt that this woman who was rejected by the aristocracy supported every step down the road that her son walked. I believe that in one way or another she is a secret to social progress in Colombia. The woman is depicted here in gray tones. It seemed fitting to the grim story of surviving a lifetime of struggle to find victory near the end of life.

**Jessica III**

This is a graphite portrait using colored pencils of a contestant in the Miss Colombia contest in 2014. She was stunningly beautiful and studied engineering at the University of Cauca in Popayan. She lost the contest that year but won in so many other ways that matter more than simply appearing attractive. She showed herself to be a dynamo of courage and determination to overcome.

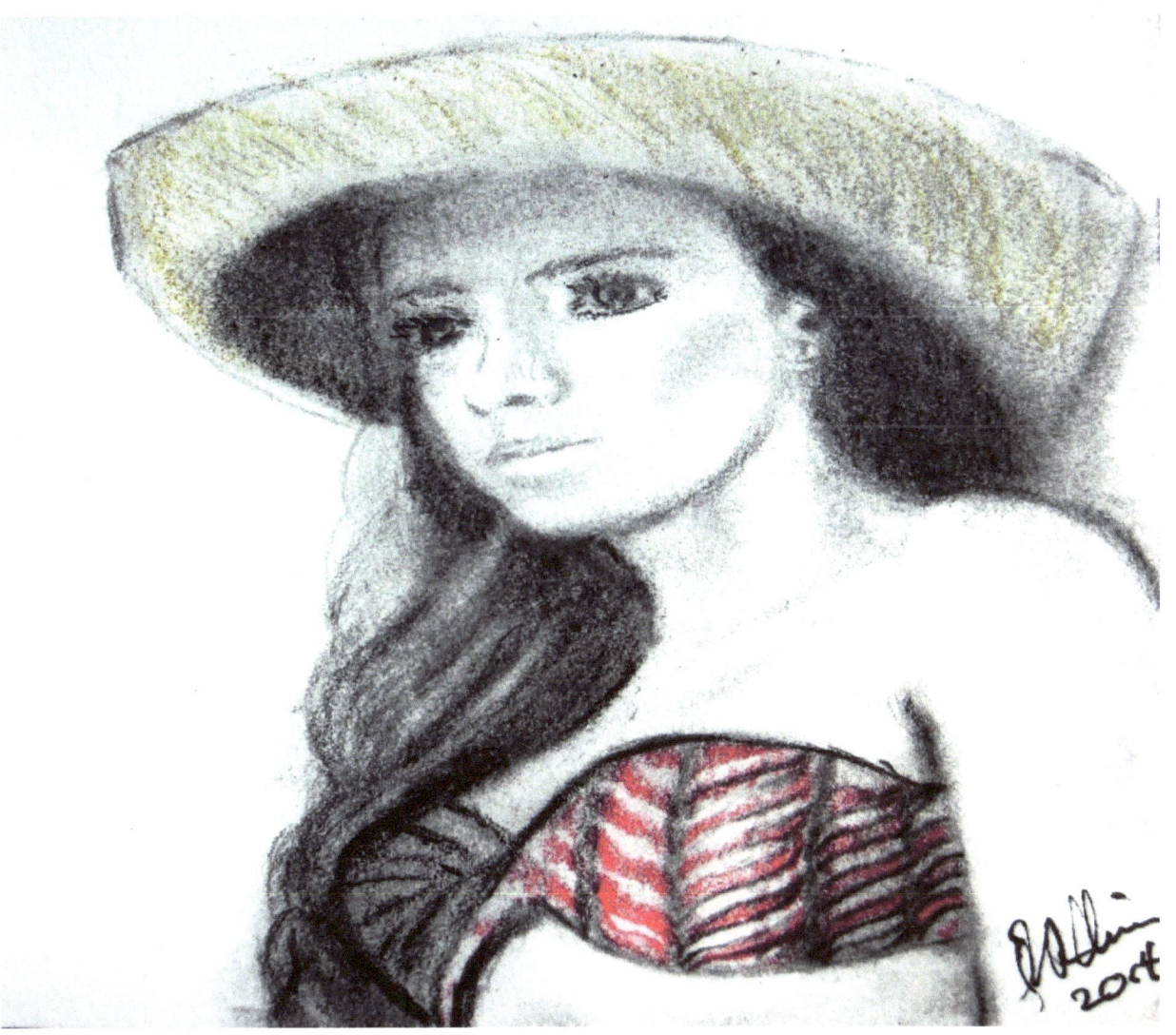

**Secretarial**

I don't know this woman's name but when I saw her on the streets in Cauca, I knew there was an iconic look about her. The belief led me to walk up and ask permission to draw her. Thankfully, she was tolerant of sketchers. I caught her for this pose during her lunch break. She made me wonder about bringing warmth to other people through showing one's comfort and confidence. I thought at the time that simply her presence would bring warmth to whomever or whatever was part of her environment.

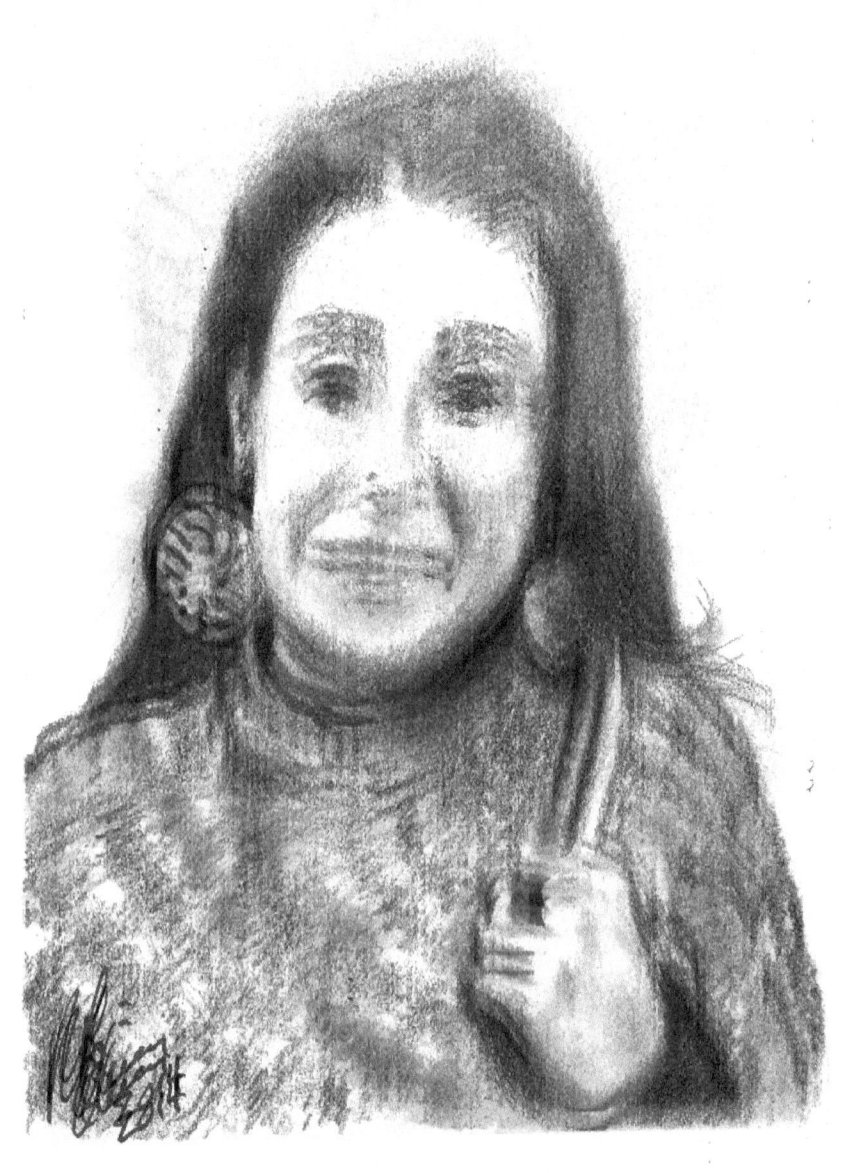

## Shorely a Penguin

A mixed media drawing that highlights a favourite animal of mine flapping its wings and pretending to fly. My experience has been that animals rejuvenate human spirits. This one immediately accomplished this purpose for me. Such images make one feel more alive.

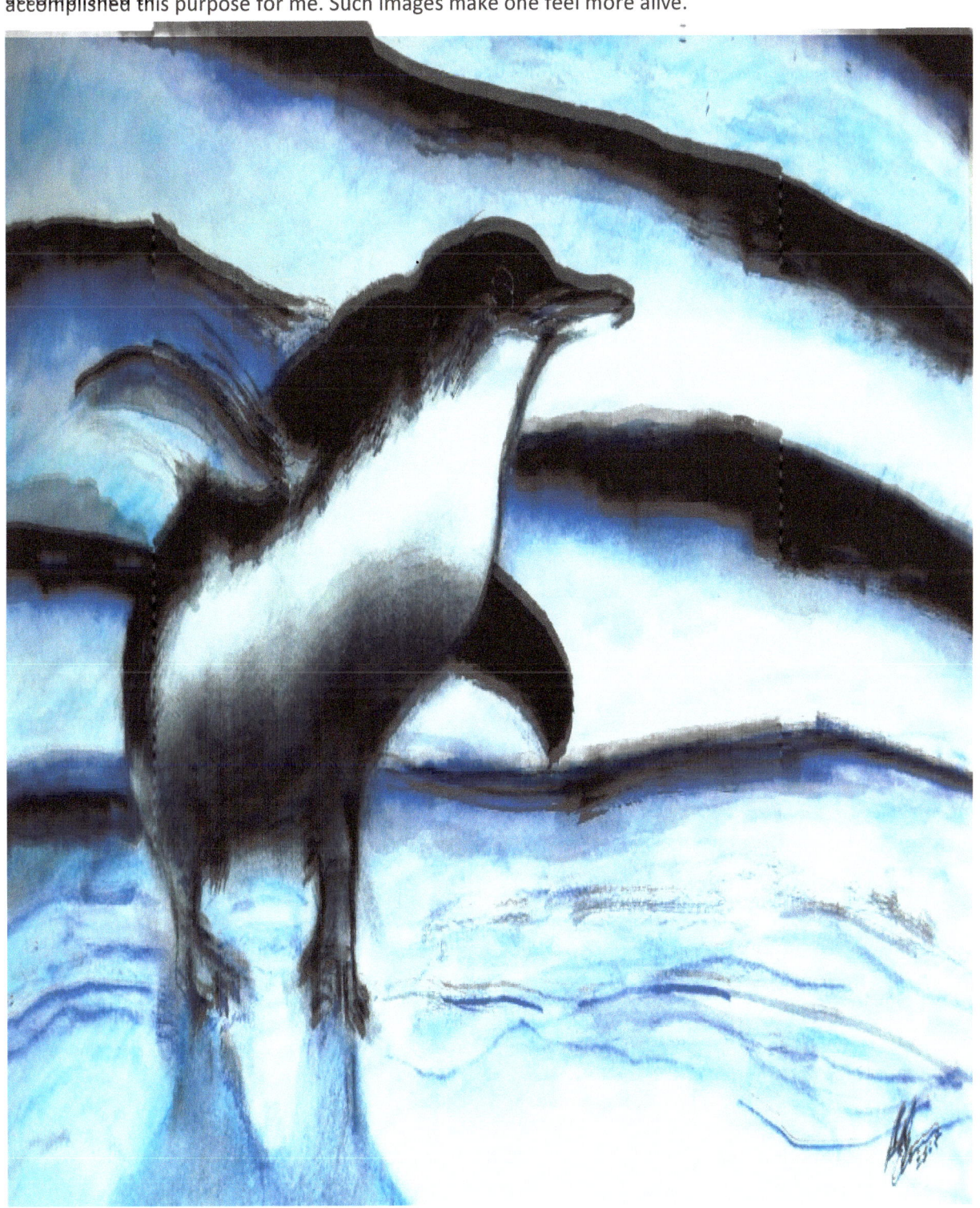

## V. Later Works

By the time I was in my forties I knew a change had to be made. I remember from the time of my early twenties being told to stay away from psychological and psychiatric professions as they were not helpful for exploration nor for making a career overture. areer. Of course, like most twenty-year-old's, I did not follow instructions or directions well and so I pursued the field it as a vocation. However, by the I was in my late forties I realized that I was swimming upstream and fighting the tide. You can swim upstream a long way but eventually you tire of the struggle. That happened to me.

Instead, I approached the challenge as a learning problem. I went back for a graduate degree in education and social psychology when I was thirty-five, I entered academia. After ten years or so of failing to gain a toehold in the academic world, I could not see the point in continuing. So, I began to ask myself the question if I needed to change gears to get me where I wanted to go? I had to admit that I was not where I wanted to be, so I adapted. I took classes in be a Nursing Assistant and basically surrendered my previous professional training. Instead, I went to work in the field of developmental disabilities which is dominated by the medical model. In my ¨artwork¨ I tried to identify: ¨What is it that needs to happen for the story to be told openly and how does the image I am drawing, or painting tell that story? Does the image serve to tie things together or pull things apart? ¨

I think of ties and connections in terms of the ¨conceptual and abstract¨. In other words, if the work has a clear message that ties us to the larger social world, I refer to it as conceptual. If it has no clearly defined connection with the larger whole, the Big Picture, I refer to it as abstract. Abstract goes beyond simple understanding and seems rooted in complexity, perplexity and the paradoxical nature of things. My path seemed to be integrating as much as possible, tying things together, whether they were recognized as parts of someone else´s world or parts of my world that needed connections.

For at least twenty years the talk in the artworld has revolved around ¨organic art¨, art that seeks to connect ourselves with ourselves and with the world at large. I knew that nature had no straight lines, and from there it was easy to think and draw in terms of roots and branches that featured curves and rounds. This curved world best represented what I saw as ¨organic¨. It did for me, and I thought it might well do the same for the viewer.

My education taught me that one has sex with the mind leading the way. Then, I thought, doesn´t nature lead the way to sex and regeneration, too? For its own sake? I tried to go beyond the individual and tie everyone to their social world. All that was needed was an image of connection that showed how things fitted together, how they went together, and how they lived together. The fierceness of survival is intrinsically a part of the organic world. Since we all like to rest in the shade, why not add shade to what you are drawing in your mind to give it a rest, to give it fluidity, to give it the needed glue to connect things together into a concept, a new way of seeing the world.

The following works are grouped together as they all seek to address the question of what makes something organic? It is a series of wet watercolor and poured acrylics. Bath trays are an essential tool if you are trying to answer this question. I officially retired in 2014 and am still looking for answers.

**Cockleburs**

I find that this work is not so much conceptual as abstract. In other words, I saw the image after I completed the creation via ink and acrylics on Yupo paper. Yupo is Japanese plastic paper that adds a new dimension to the watercolor dynamic. I called it cocklebur after seeing all the spines on the outer borders, much like the form of a seed dispersal system that adheres to whatever brushes against it to carry to a new field where it can be sown afresh for regeneration. It is a poured watercolor with the only thought given being that the color selection mattered most. This was the start of an experimentation process work that yielded some visually stimulating and fascinating images, I thought.

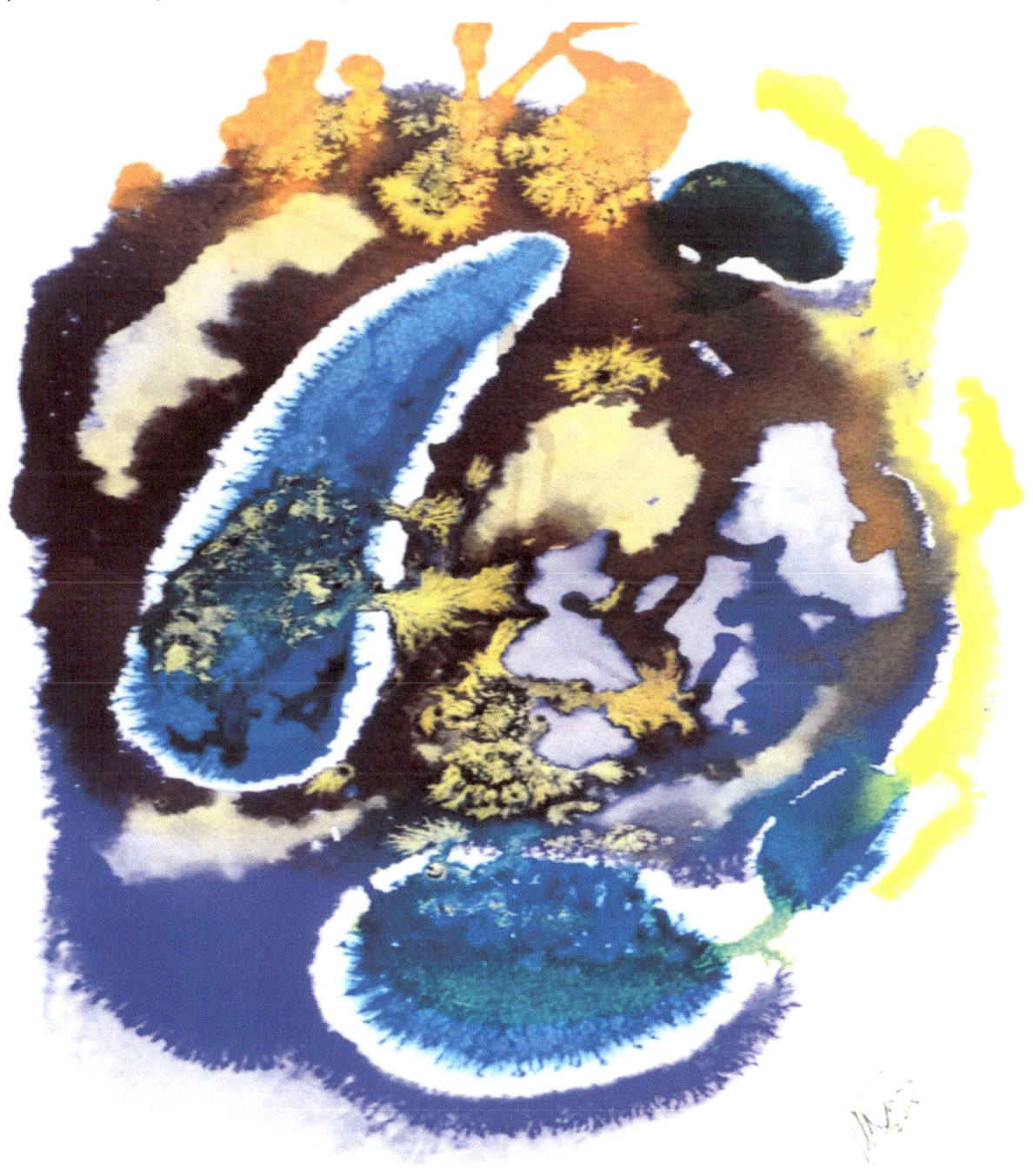

**Rainbow Sprouts:**

This one was named Rainbow Sprouts as it looked vibrant and intensely alive… much like a germinating, rootbound seed that wanted only to grow and shoot off new beginnings. What I found so fulfilling and fascinating in this work is that it uses a wet method of mixing water on a wet surface where you never know what the final result will be until you let it dry overnight and see it for the first time at the start of a new day. It can leave you with a warm feeling inside knowing that you are forming original images from waterworks. It all becomes visible only after a night of forming and growing and arranging its presentation. It is not an immediate image but only shows itself after you give it time to form during the night.

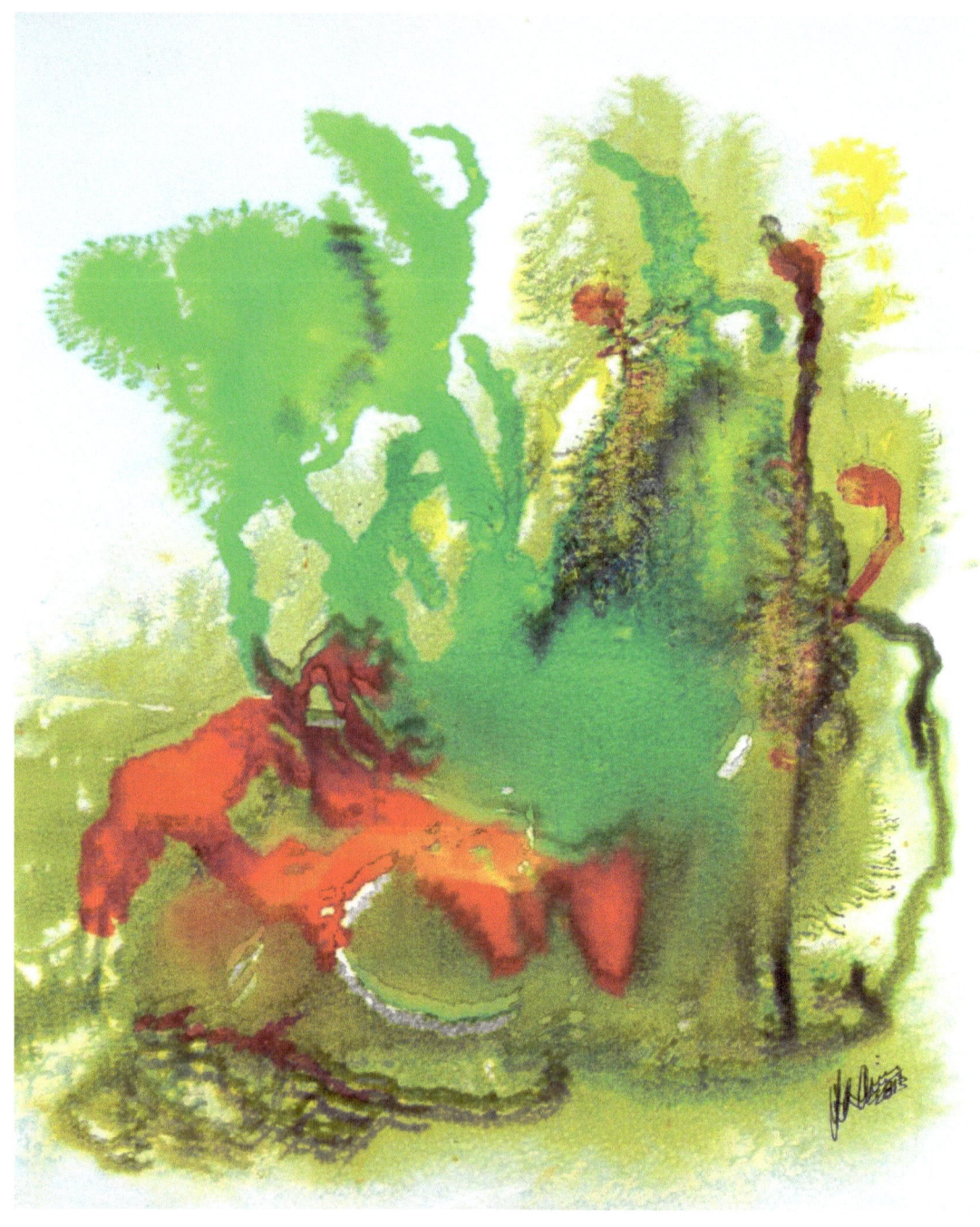

# Rooted in Randomness

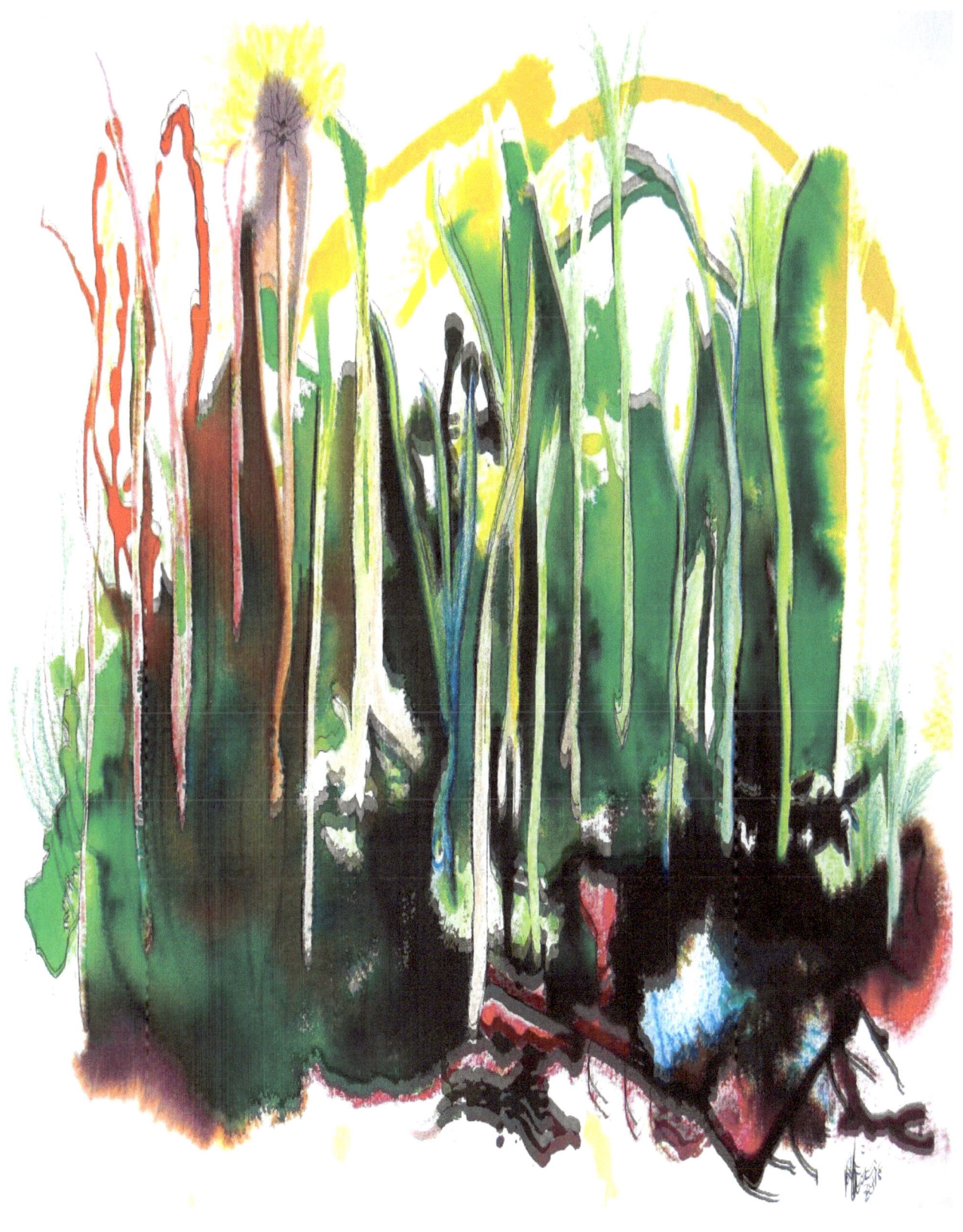

**Rooted in Whimsy - 2015**

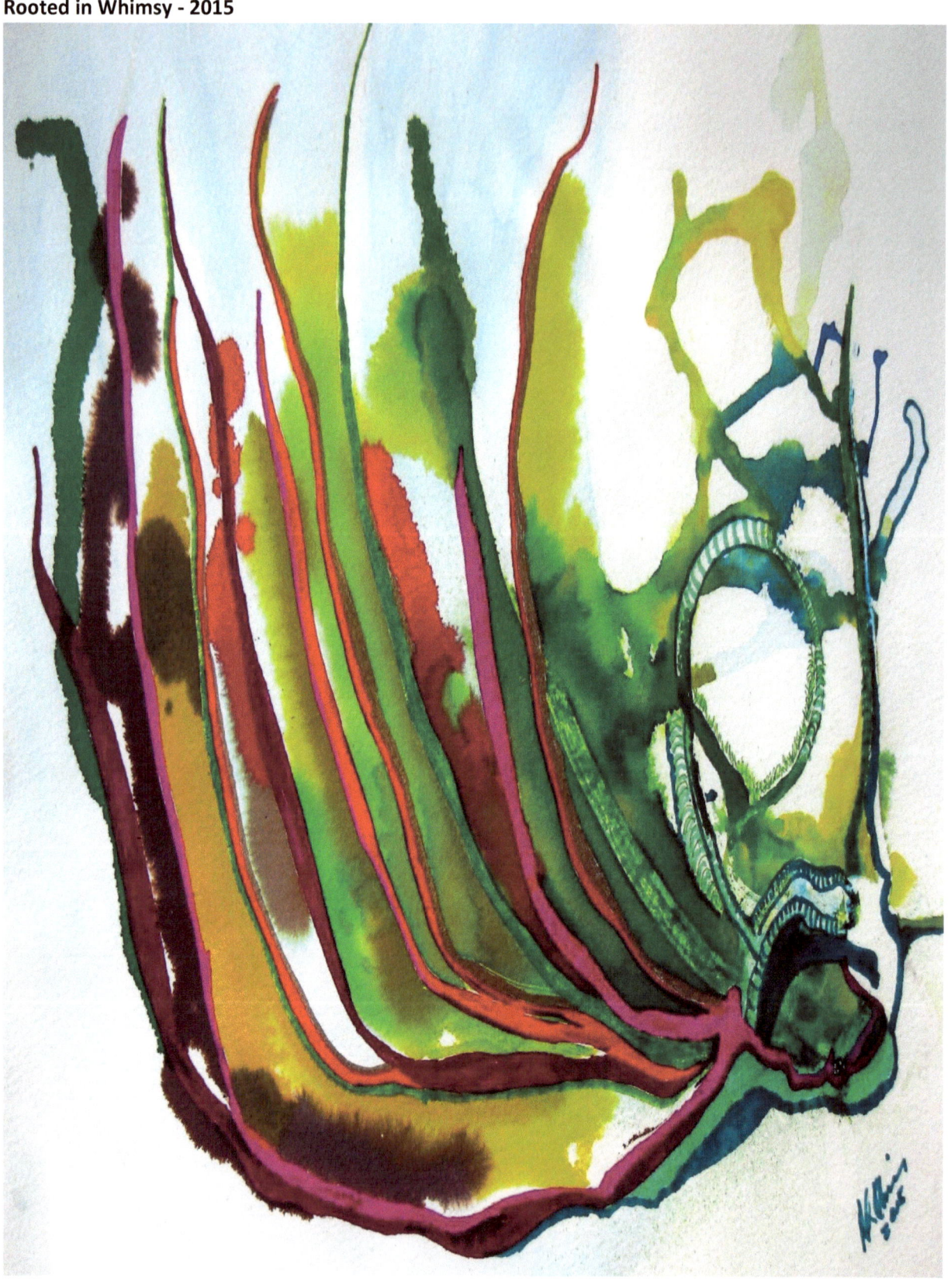

**Fire in the Belly 2015**

This works grew from the idea that art inspiration was like passion that glowed like a fire in the belly. That is, it grew naturally over time and came to dominate both will and reason in the name of desire and want, i.e. passion. The process simply grows and grows larger and larger in size and scope until in the end it is the only thing that matters. It was with this work that I began experimenting with the use of oil and wax pastels of color that were much easier to manipulate by finger than by brush. In this work they were combined with salt for effect. This work is about 3 feet by 4 feet in size.

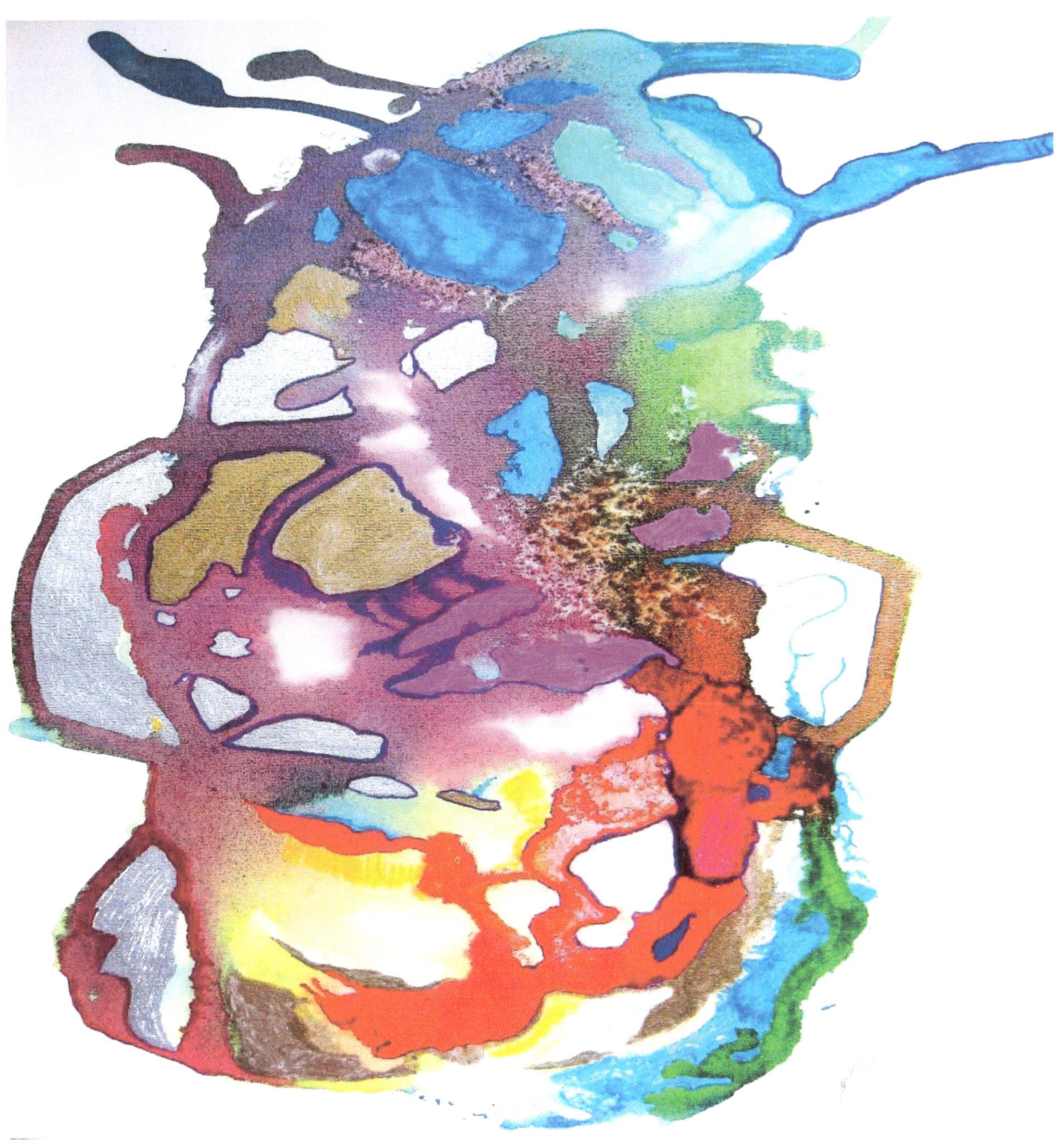

Crayon Jungle

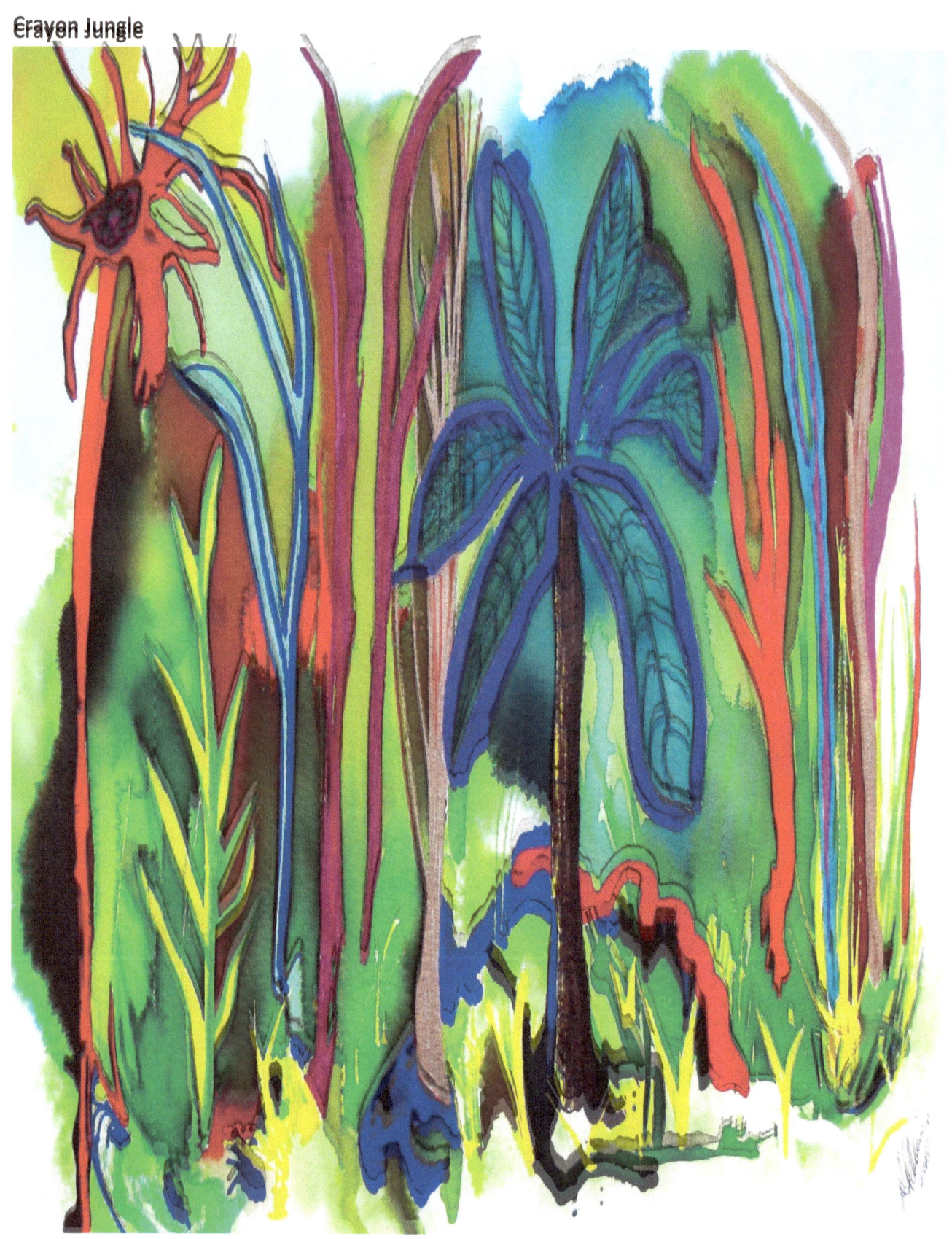

# Flaming Bananas

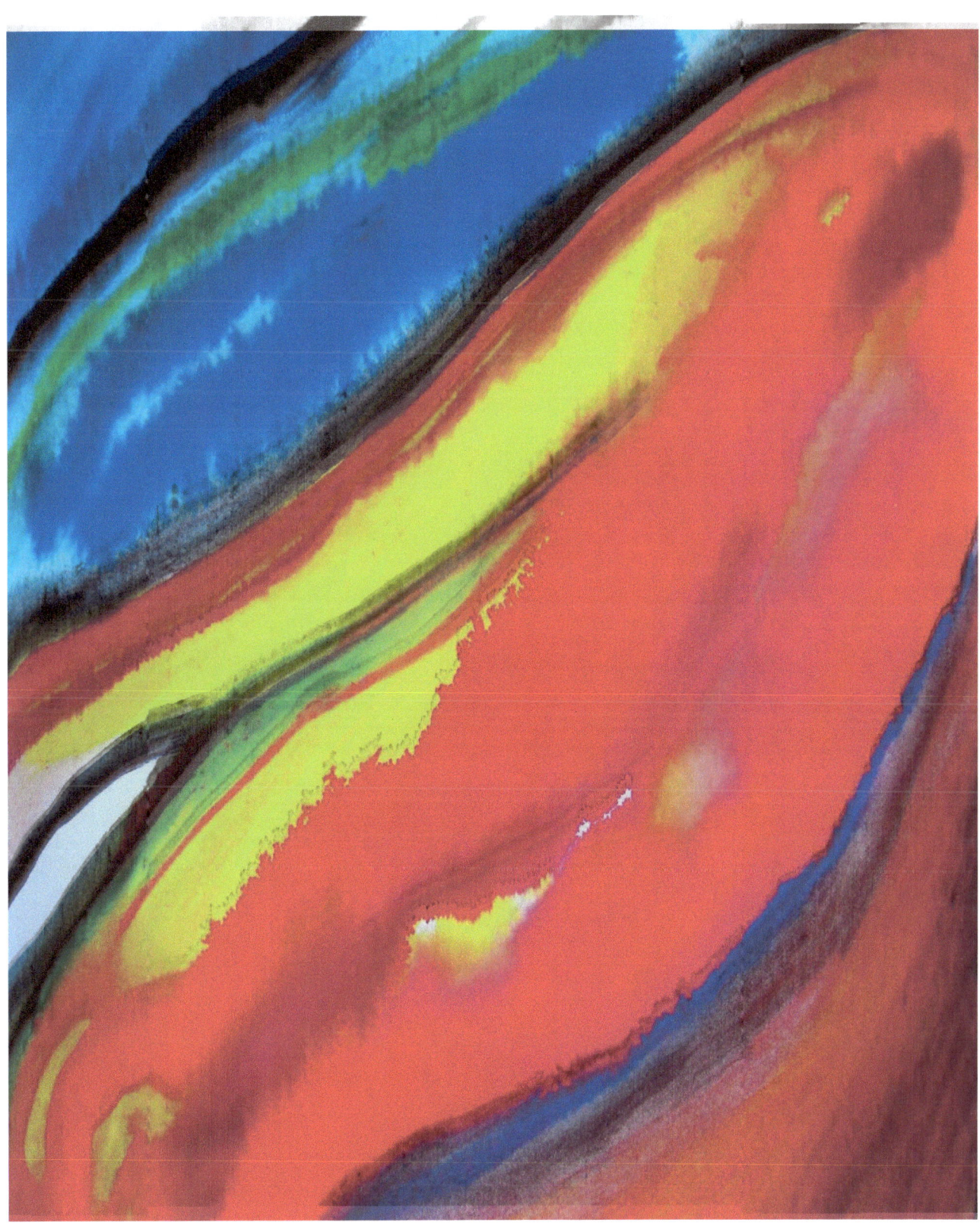

**Cerebral Roots**

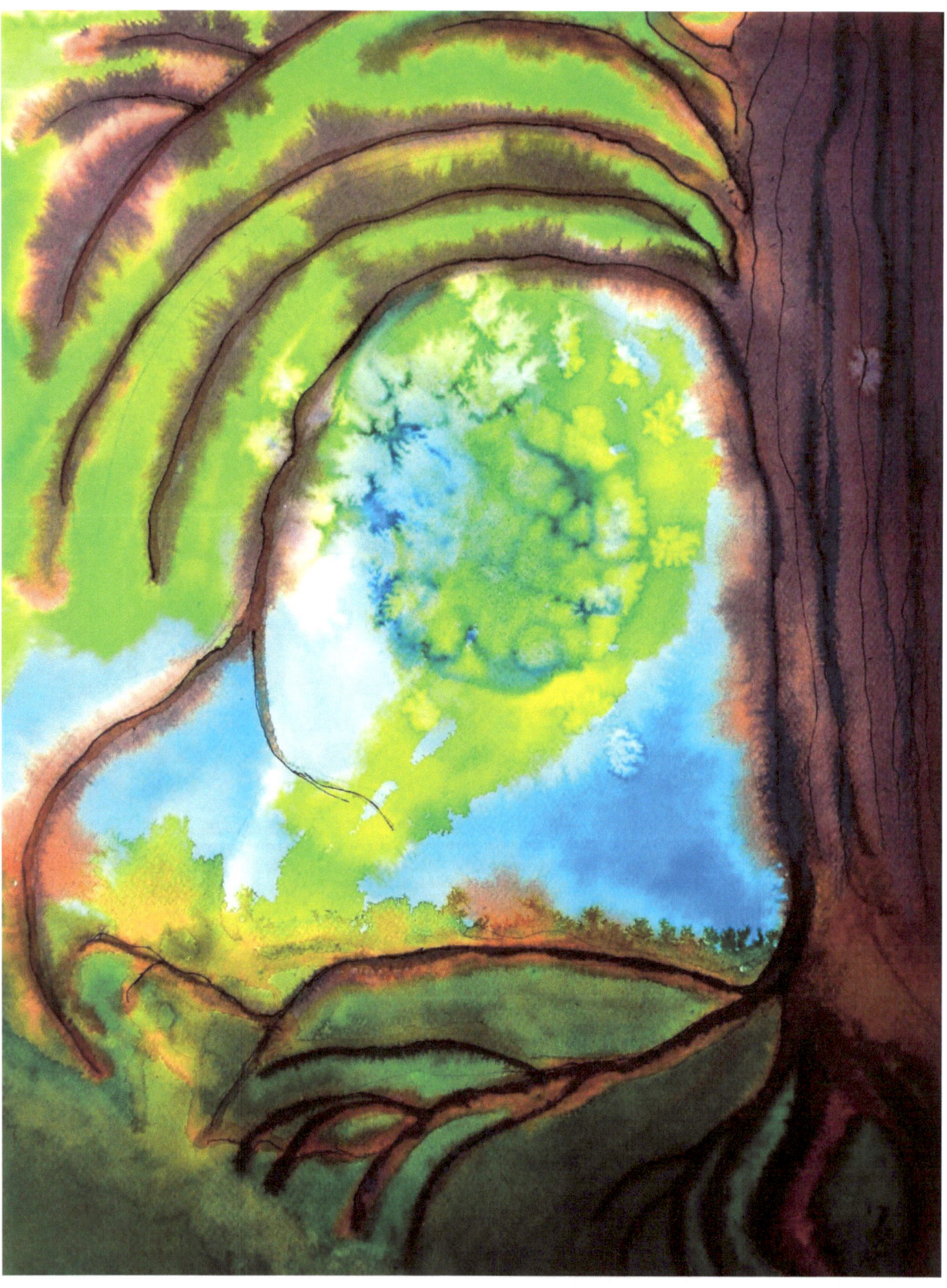

**Disintegration**

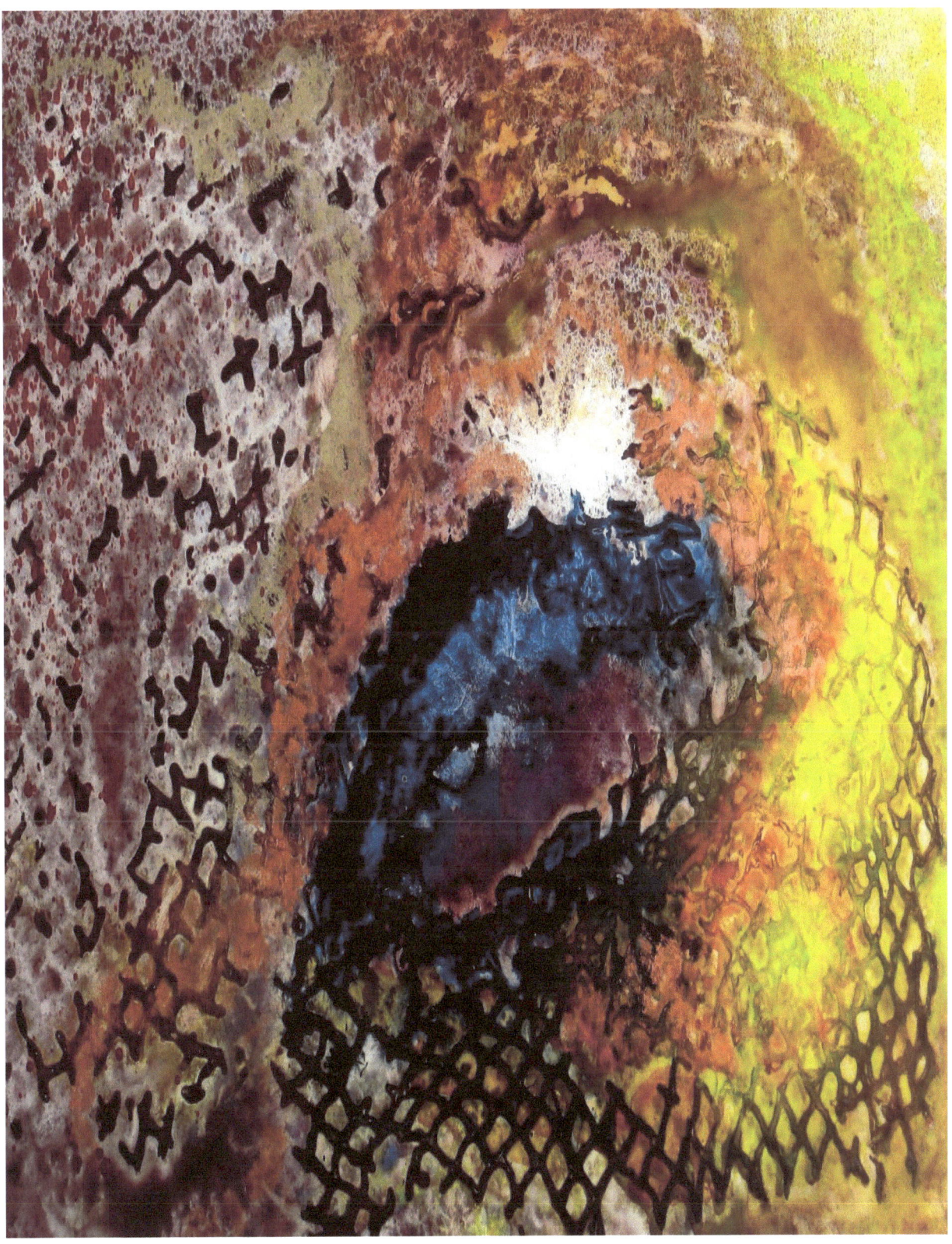

# Primordial Growth

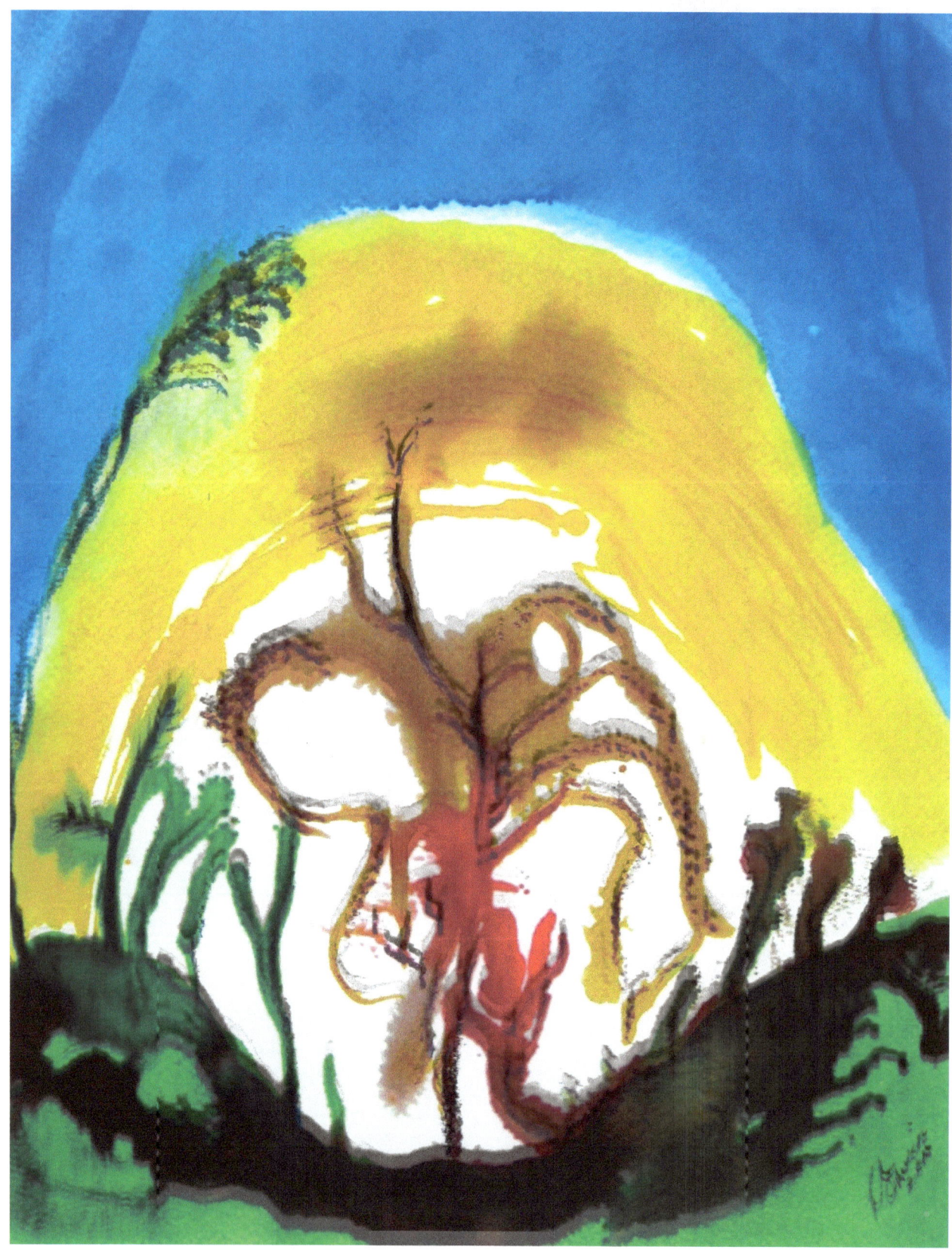

# Dissolving World

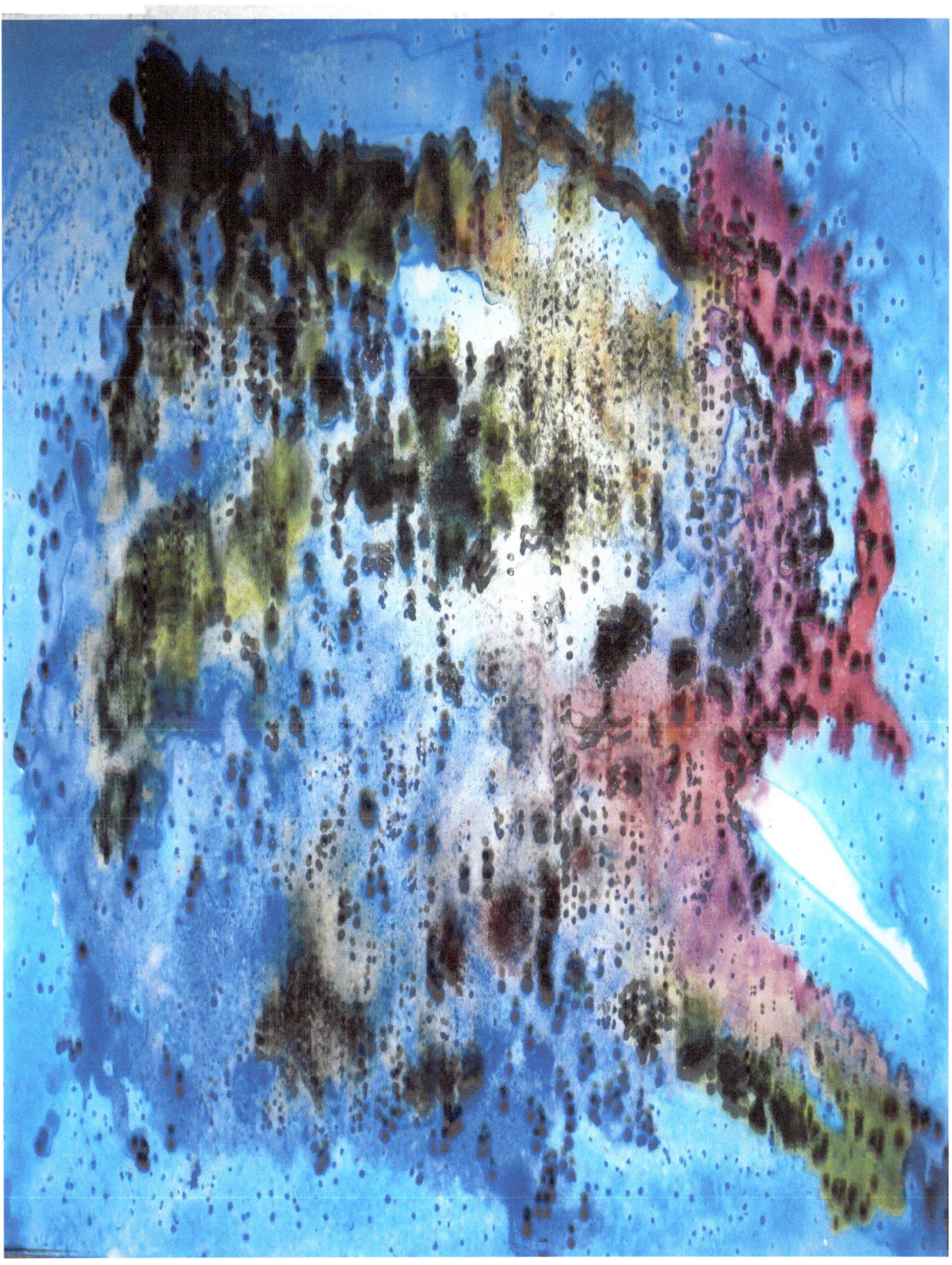

**A Rock Just Told**

This image was taken from the book of poetry I wrote called If Dirt Could Talk. The work was originally done on plastic paper that has unusual and distinctive drying patterns. I found it difficult to imagine a rock that talked but after exploring all of nature, both solid and liquid, it became much easier to imagine and work with.

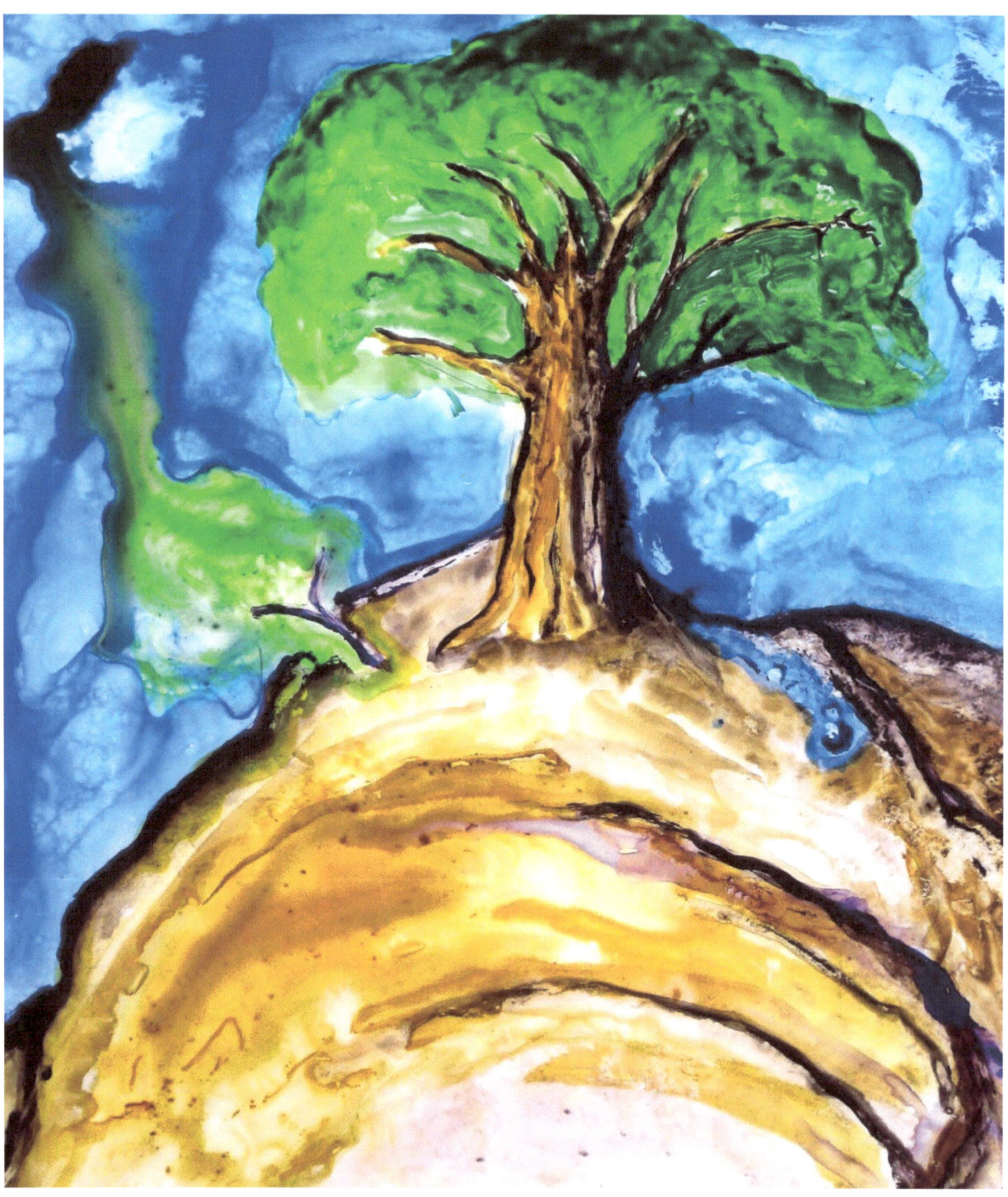

**Pensando en Agua 2017**

This work is an amalgamation of ideas. First, I took a Cuban contemplator sitting on the dirt outside his home in Havana and transplanted him to San Francisco Bay. This goes along with the theme of integration that I adopted. All the while, I imagined, the man was thinking about the sorry disrespect we show water everywhere, and yet it is a source of all life. When you stop and think about it, it makes no kind of sense at all! Where do we come up with such a will to treat life this way? It is something worth thinking about and one I imagined this man considered regularly.

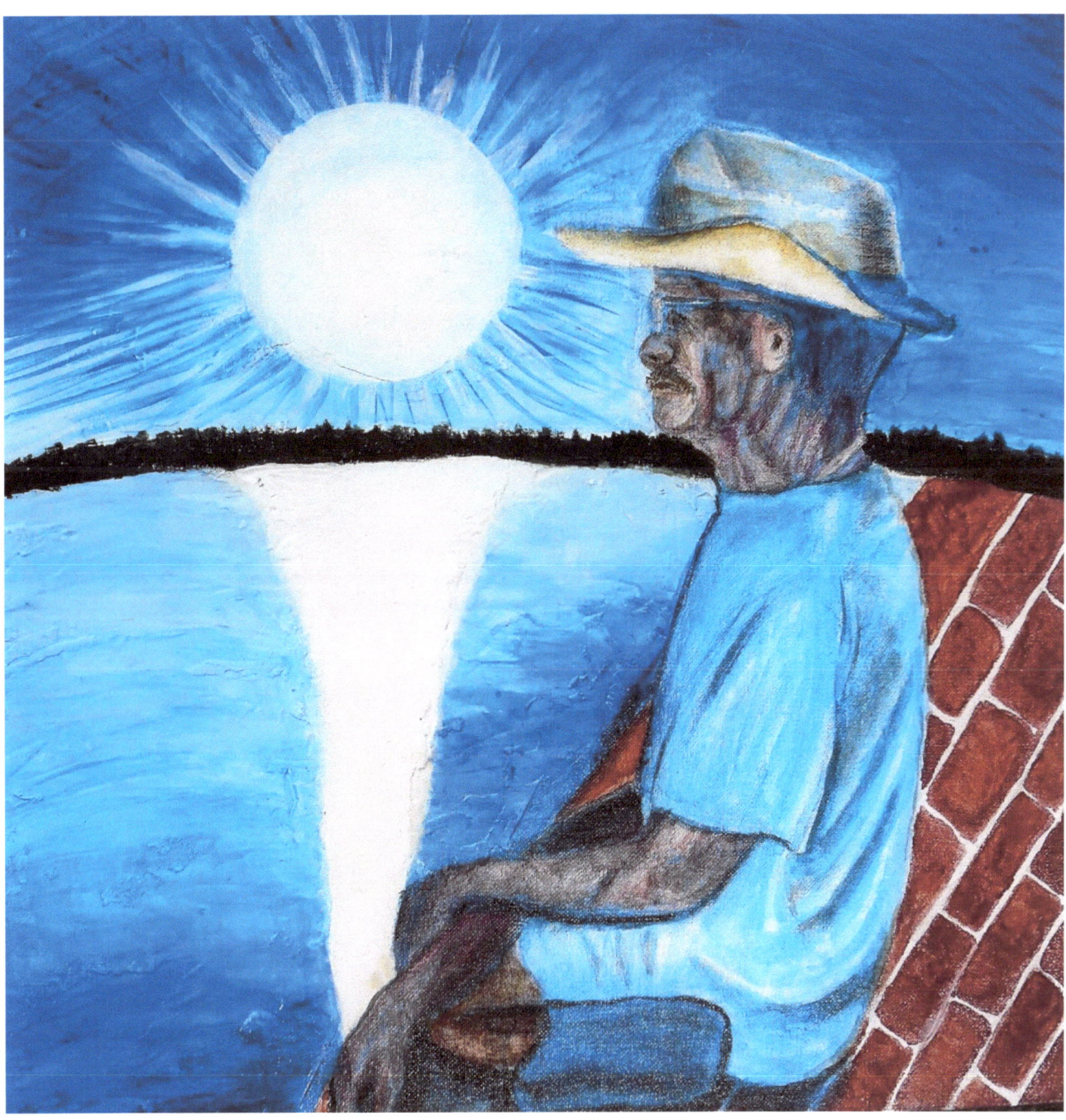

# Cafetero

## 2017

This is a conceptual work that puts the figure where he belongs --- in a field growing one of the basics of life, coffee. I would say that Juan Valdez who is an imaginary would look much like the figure in the image. He has become part of the Colombian psyche and therefore its national identity. He is seen so much on commercials and ads that he is much like a national hero in Colombia. You can tell by the name of Colombian Football Team: they are known as the Cafeteros.

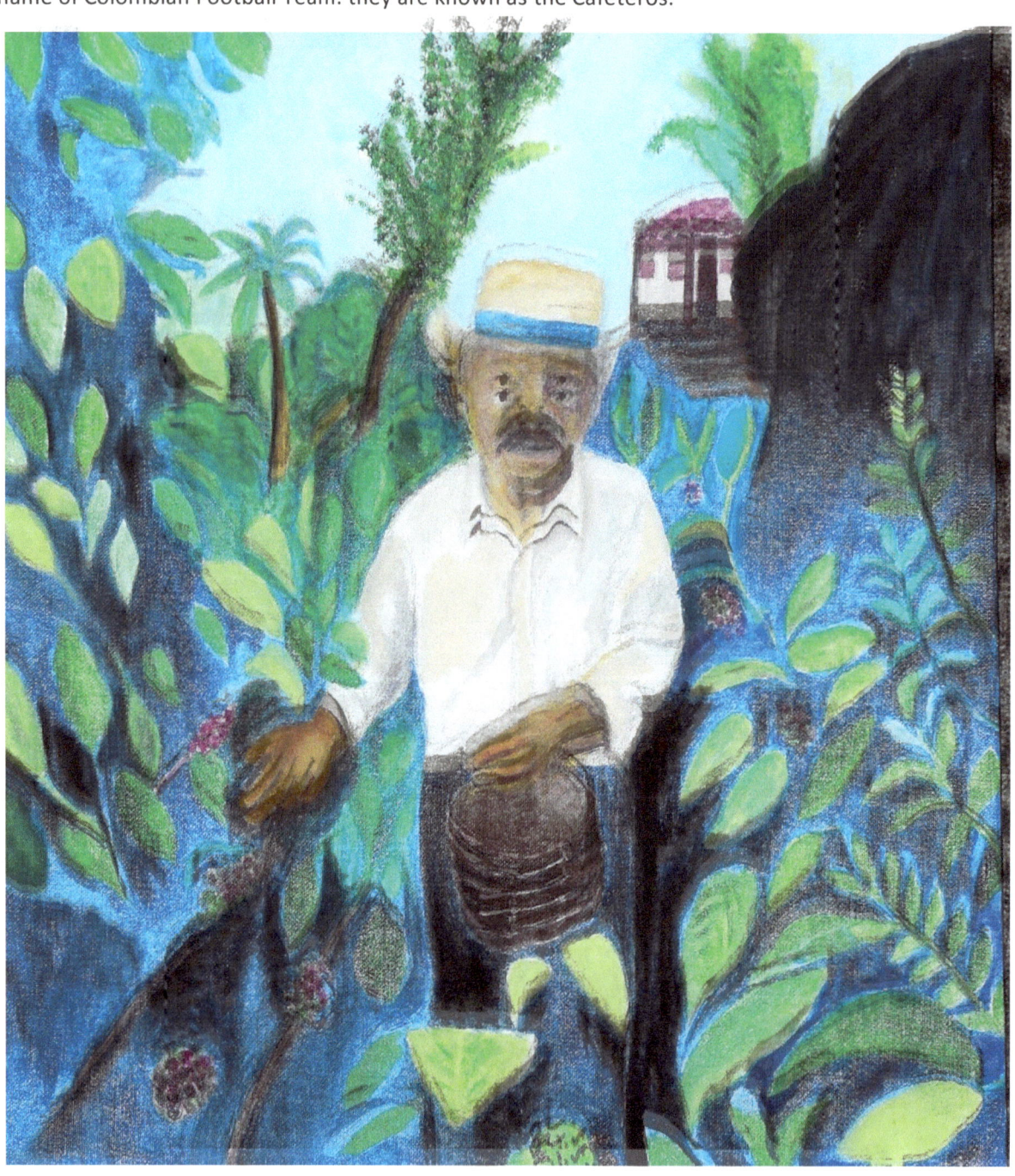

# Quechuan Aguatero

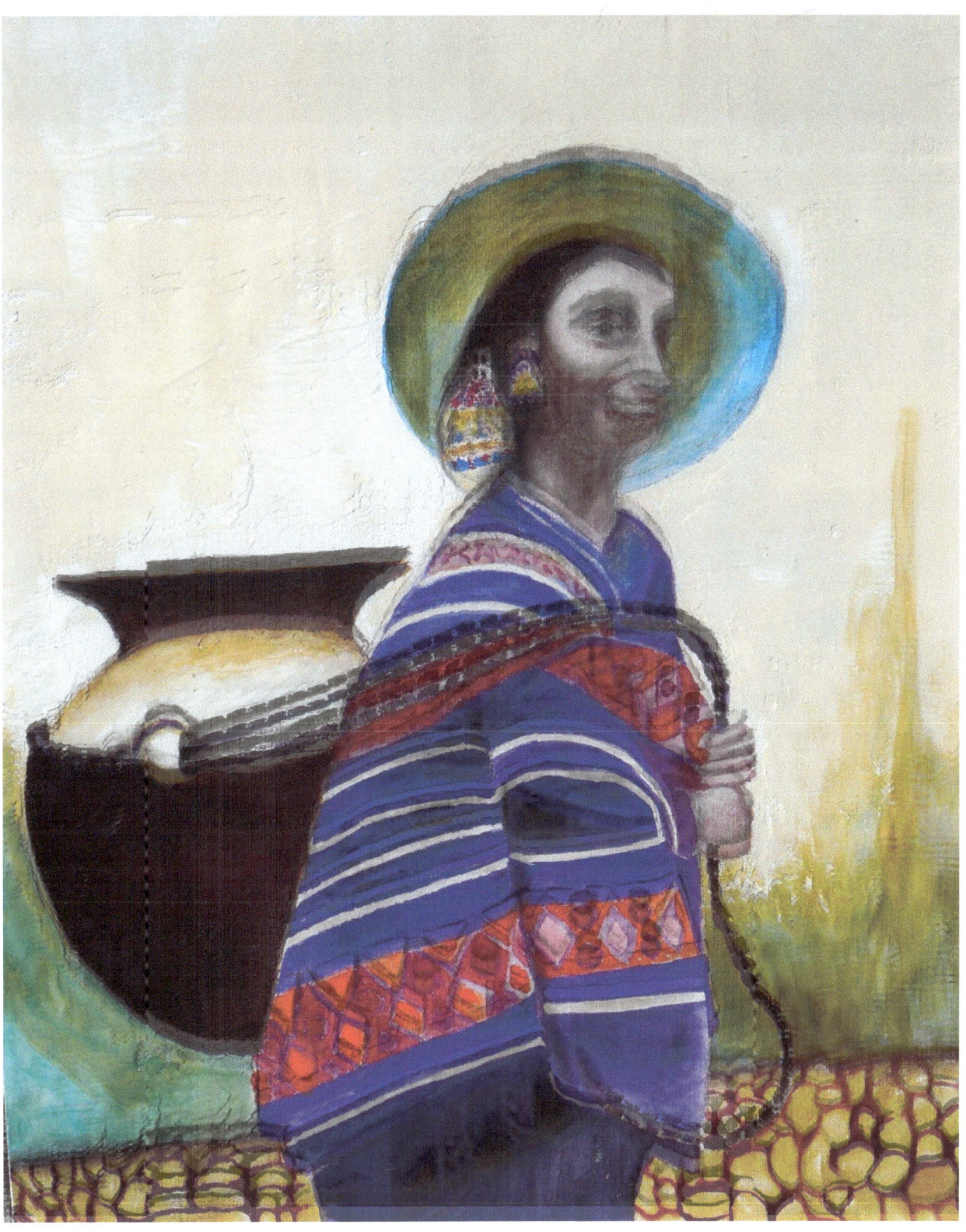

## VI. The Here and Now

### Alone Again Naturally

This was done with graphite and charcoal much like I used in my earliest works. I see this as an indication that I am coming full circle. It has taken most of a lifetime, but it is so. I do have a sense of completion, which is most fulfilling. The image below was taken from a UNICEF agenda book of 1990 and is of a Mexican child gripped in her feelings of being alone and lonely. We can all relate to that.

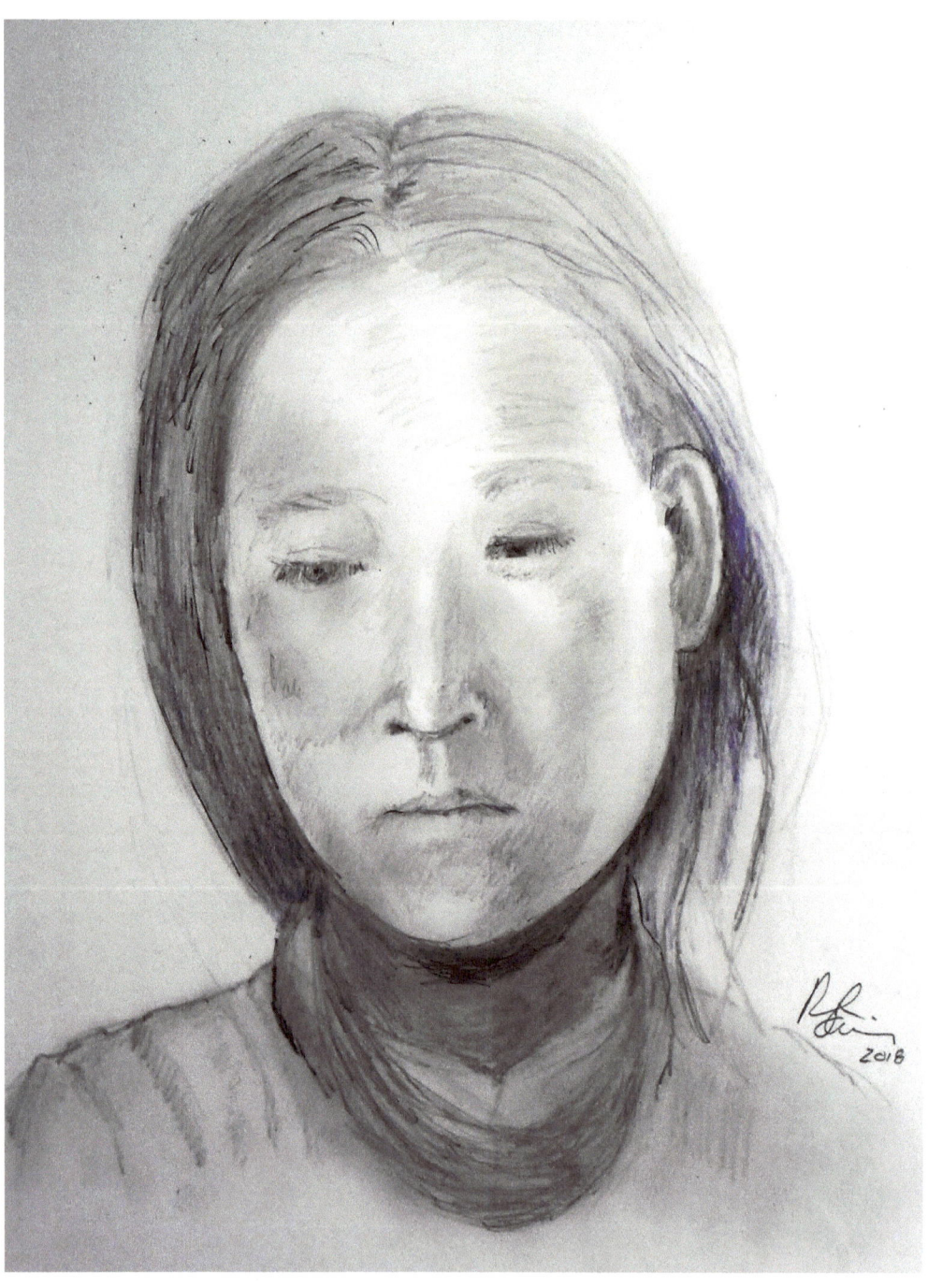

**Girl from the Philippines**

This was again done with graphite on Bristol Board paper. I got to the point where I only wanted to use the best paper possible out of respect for the subject matter. When I first posted this online, I got a reply from a fellow artist who remarked, ¨You know, I can´t seem to keep my eyes from her... she captivates. ¨ Yes, I couldn´t take my eyes from her, either. That´s seems to say that it is truly art... the inability to escape the beautiful.

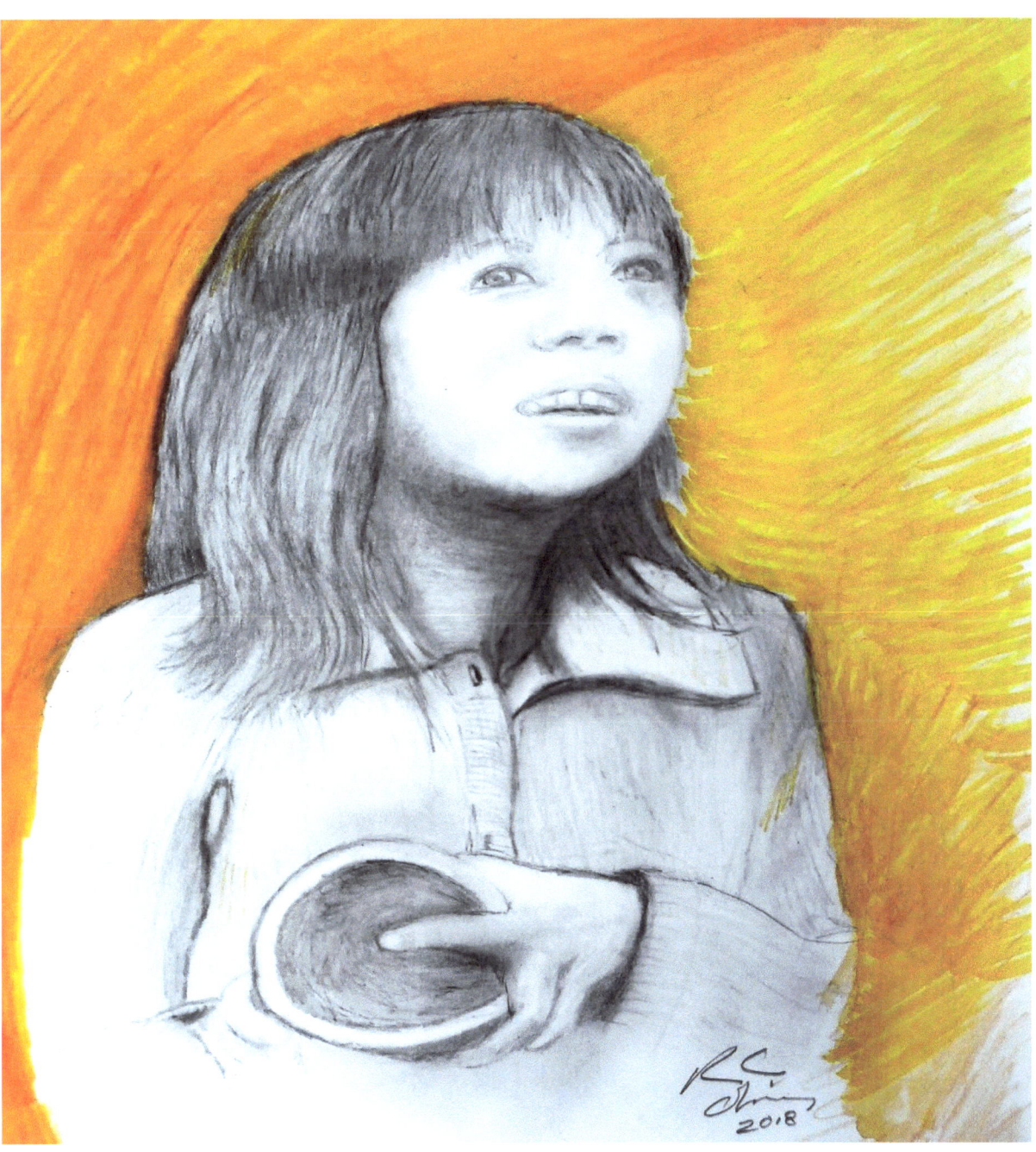

## Watermelon Shade

I want to leave with a sense of beginning. I have found that there is nothing better than a shade tree and a slice of watermelon. It is there for you to eat and enjoy while resting in the shade. This drawing is another self-portrait with me being the barefooted boy on the left at about five years of age. I am grateful for many good memories of childhood that mostly involve growing up under a heaven of treetops. It is a good place for older folks, too. Drawing can put you there.

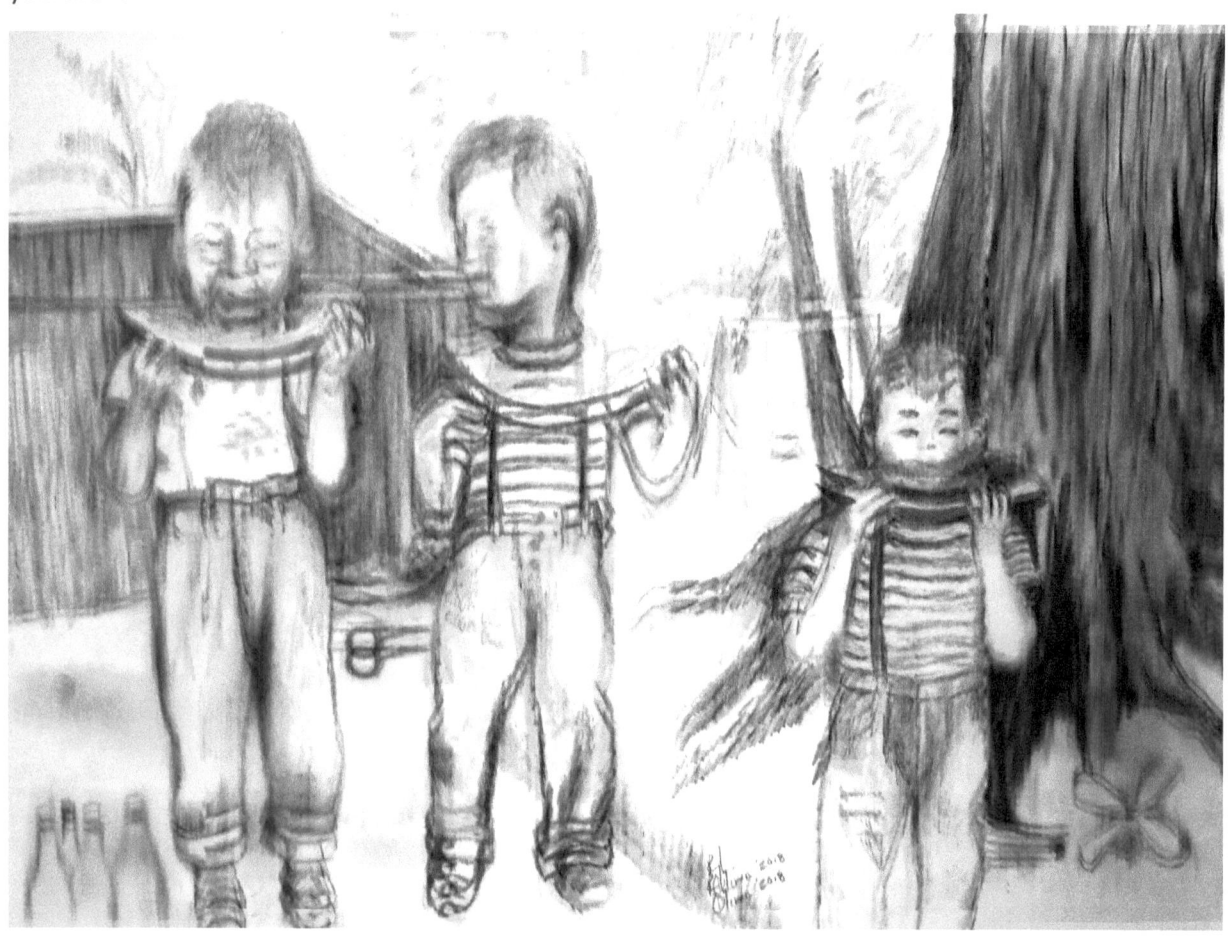

**Endnote**: I discovered that all helping professionals suffer from burn out from time to time and it leaves them questioning their choices, identity, and sanity. It seems to me, that giving too much is not an insane or worrisome thing. Calling it a "mental health problem" is offensive to me as we all suffer periodically from this fate. It is the way things are, a fact of life. Surely one day we will all learn that and find ways to better accept ourselves and reality.

### THE END

**Back Cover: Golden Rubber Tree of Dog Park** mixed media on canvas

# Appendix A
## List of Illustrations

| Name | Date | Media | Reference |
|---|---|---|---|
| 1. Walker's Girl | 1969 | Graphite on paper | p. 5 |
| 2. Country Doctor | 1969 | Graphite on paper | p. 6 |
| 3. James Baldwin | 1969 | Graphite on paper | p. 8 |
| 4. Jimi Hendrix | 1969 | Graphite & Charcoal on paper | p. 9 |
| 5. Abe | 1976 | Charcoal on paper | p. 10 |
| 6. A Neighbour | 1976 | Graphite on paper | p. 11 |
| 7. Self Portrait | 1978 | Graphite on paper | p. 12 |
| 8. Moon Over Melissa | 1981 | Graphite on paper | p. 13 |
| 9. A Man and Dog or Tramp on the Street | 1981 | Graphite and charcoal on paper | p. 14 |
| 10. Self Portrait | 1982 | Graphite on paper | p. 16 |
| 11. Young Cowboys | 1982 | Ink and graphite on paper | p. 17 |
| 12. Little Miss Music | 1988 | Charcoal on paper | p. 18 |
| 13. Holding Tight | 1989 | Graphite on paper | p. 19 |
| 14. Melissa | 1989 | Graphite on paper | p. 20 |
| 15. After Vermeer | 1994 | Acrylics on canvas | p. 21 |
| 16. Yellowstone Fire | 1989 | Pastels on paper | p. 22 |
| 17. Walking into Darkness | 1991 | Ink on paper | p. 23 |
| 18. Grandfather Winston | 1994 | Graphite on paper | p. 25 |
| 19. Grandmother Nellie Wave | 1994 | Graphite on paper | p. 26 |
| 20. Big Grins | 1995 | Pastels on paper | p. 27 |
| 21. Still Life with Limes | 1995 | Acrylics on canvas | p. 28 |
| 22. Madonna and Child | 1996 | Graphite on paper | p. 29 |
| 23. Smell This | 1996 | Chalk Pastels on paper | p. 30 |
| 24. The Child in the Basement | 1996 | Graphite and pastels on paper | p. 31 |
| 25. The Searcher | 1996 | Pastels on paper | p. 32 |
| 26. Colorado | 1997 | Acrylics on canvas | p. 33 |
| 27. A Cabin in the Pines | 1989 | Pastels on paper | p. 34 |
| 28. Abstract #161 | 1996 | Mixed pastels on paper | p. 35 |

| # | Title | Year | Medium | Page |
|---|---|---|---|---|
| 29. | Drawing Mother | 1997 | Graphite on paper | p. 36 |
| 30. | Yellow Maraca | 2013 | Watercolor on paper | p. 37 |
| 31. | Flor Bromelia | 2014 | Watercolor & glycerin on paper | p. 38 |
| 32. | Let´s Go Fly a Bike | 2014 | Mixed Media on paper | p. 39 |
| 33. | Colombian Girl in Yumbo | 2014 | Watercolor on paper | p. 40 |
| 34. | Crying Campesino | 2015 | Watercolor on paper | p. 41 |
| 35. | Displaced | 2014 | Watercolor on paper | p. 42 |
| 36. | Silletero Feliz | 2014 | Watercolor on paper | p. 43 |
| 37. | Washerwoman Mother | 2014 | Graphite on paper | p. 44 |
| 38. | Jessica III | 2014 | Graphite and pastel on paper | p. 45 |
| 39. | Secretarial | 2017 | Graphite on paper | p. 46 |
| 40. | Shorely a Penguin | 2015 | Mixed media on paper | p. 47 |
| 41. | Cockleburs | 2015 | Ink and watercolor on paper | p. 49 |
| 42. | Rainbow Sprouts | 2015 | Ink and watercolor on paper | p. 50 |
| 43. | Rooted in Random | 2015 | Mixed media on paper | p. 51 |
| 44. | Rooted in Whimsy | 2015 | Mixed media on paper | p. 52 |
| 45. | Fire in the Belly | 2015 | Mixed media on canvas | p. 53 |
| 46. | Crayon Jungle | 2015 | Mixed media on paper | p. 54 |
| 47. | Flaming Bananas | 2015 | Mixed media on paper | p. 55 |
| 48. | Cerebral Roots | 2016 | Watercolor on paper | p. 56 |
| 49. | Disintegration | 2016 | Mixed media on paper | p. 57 |
| 50. | Primordial Growth | 2016 | Mixed media on paper | p. 58 |
| 51. | Dissolving World | 2016 | Mixed media on paper | p. 59 |
| 52. | A Rock Just Told | 2017 | Watercolor on Yupo paper | p. 60 |
| 53. | Pensando en Agua | 2017 | Mixed media on canvas | p. 61 |
| 54. | Cafetero | 2018 | Mixed media on canvas | p. 62 |
| 55. | Quechuan Aguatero | 2017 | Mixed media on canvas | p. 63 |
| 56. | Alone Again, Naturally | 2018 | Graphite on paper | p. 64 |
| 57. | Girl from the Philippines | 2018 | Mixed media on paper | p. 65 |
| 58. | Watermelon Shade | 2018 | Graphite & charcoal on paper | p. 66 |
| 59. | Golden Rubber Tree of Dog Park | 2018 | Mixed media on canvas | 69 and back cover |

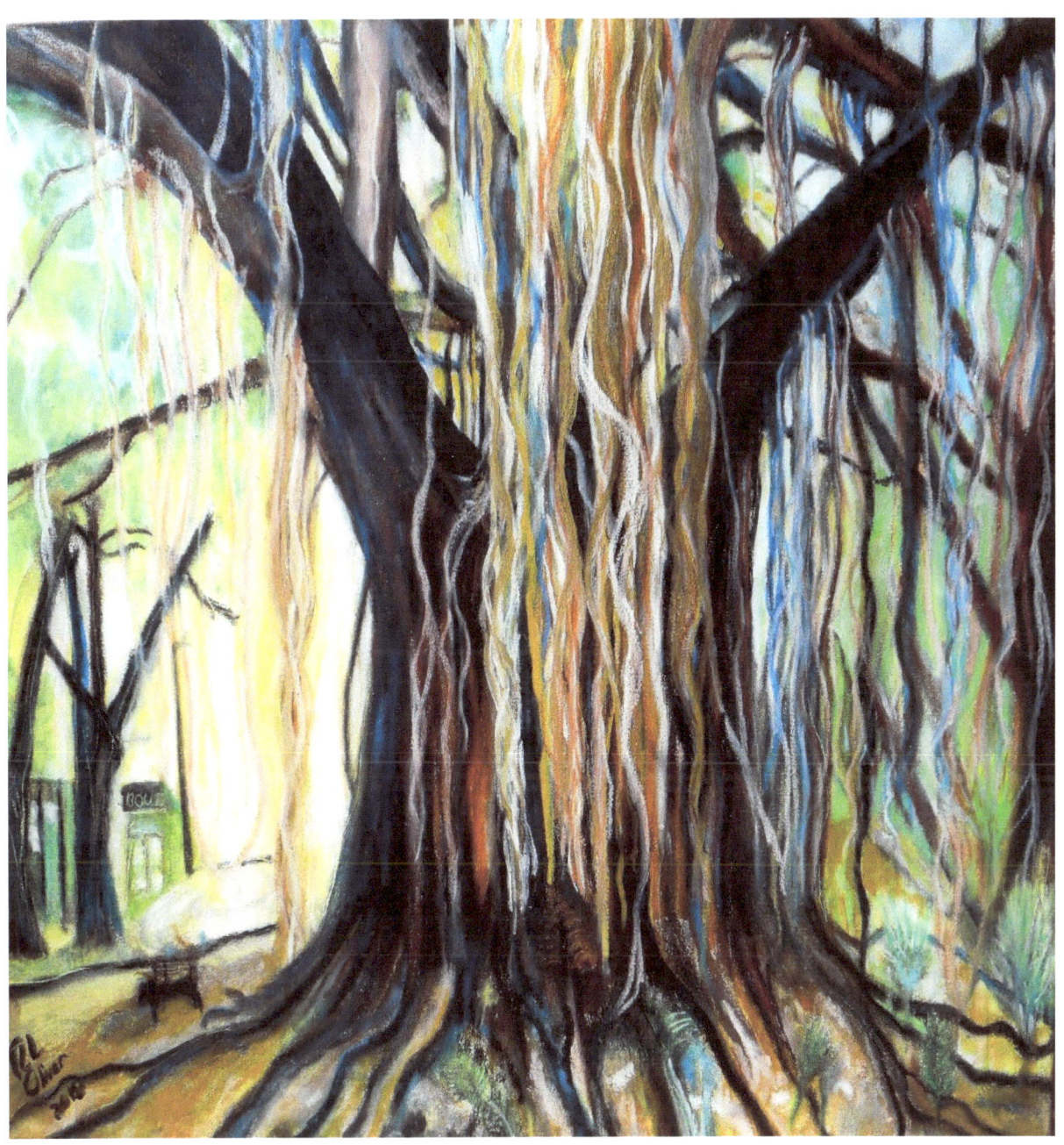

www.ingramcontent.com/pod-product-compliance
Lightning Source LLC
Chambersburg PA
CBHW051918210526
45473CB00006B/2053